LATIMER BRIEFING 12

PREACHING

A Guidebook for Beginners

By Allan Chapple

The Latimer Trust

Preaching: A Guidebook for Beginners © Allan Chapple 2013

ISBN   978-1-906327-14-9

Cover photo: Studying the Word of God © georgemuresan - Fotolia.com

Bible references are taken from The Holy Bible, New International Version®, NIV® Copyright © 1973, 1978, 1984, 2011 by Biblica, Inc.™ Used by permission. All rights reserved worldwide.

Published by the Latimer Trust February 2013

The Latimer Trust (formerly Latimer House, Oxford) is a conservative Evangelical research organisation within the Church of England, whose main aim is to promote the history and theology of Anglicanism as understood by those in the Reformed tradition. Interested readers are welcome to consult its website for further details of its many activities.

The Latimer Trust
c/o Oak Hill College
London N14 4PS UK
Registered Charity: 1084337
Company Number: 4104465
Web: www.latimertrust.org
E-mail: administrator@latimertrust.org

Like all authors, I have accumulated some debts that should be acknowledged.

The guinea pigs on whom the material in this book was tried out have been the students at Trinity Theological College. I am grateful for their feedback, and for the encouragement and support of our Principal, the Reverend Doctor Don West.

I am also grateful to the following friends for their help and encouragement along the way: Paul Barnett, Peter Brain, Mike Fischer, Derek Jones, and Kanishka Raffel. Margaret Hobbs of the Latimer Trust has made the process of producing this book amazingly smooth and trouble-free.

I could not have done the teaching and writing that led to this book without the constant loving support of my wife Allison. This book is dedicated to her, with deep thanks.

Allan Chapple

January 2013

Introduction

This book is not meant to cover every aspect of preaching. It is a manual for beginners. By the time you finish it you should be well on the way to behaving as every preacher should, instinctively reaching out for the clearest, simplest ways of communicating the Bible's message.

Unless beginners have been exposed to good models of preaching, they are often unsure about what to do and how to do it. Many otherwise good books on preaching concentrate on spelling out the principles, wrongly assuming that the practice will then take care of itself. What is needed is not just a textbook on the theory, but a guidebook that gives plenty of detail about the practice as well. That is what this book is for.

We preachers need to keep working hard at developing our skills (1 Timothy 4:13-16). One useful way of doing this is to read a book on preaching every year. This is likely to remind us of important matters we have been neglecting; it might also introduce us to worthwhile approaches we had not previously considered. Even if it does not teach us anything new, it will have proved its value if it helps us to stay on track and encourages us to keep going. That is one reason I have written this book.

I have been preaching for nearly fifty years, and have always regarded it as a very important ministry. As a result, I have tried to learn as much as I could from other preachers, by listening to their preaching, or by talking to them about it, or by reading their books. Some of what I have learned during these years now seems obvious – but more often than not, it wasn't obvious to me until after I had heard it or read it for the first time. Some of it had a profound effect on me when I first encountered it, and is still basic to my whole understanding and practice of preaching. Some of it is not as important to me now as it used to be, and conversely, some is more important to me now than it once was. When I came to gather all of this material together, I discovered that there was quite a lot of it. I thought there was a good chance that some of it would help others as it has helped me, and so this book came into being.

I have included many quotations in this book. Some say things I disagree with and some disagree with each other. This is not intended to be confusing, but to help readers think their way through the issues until they reach their own convictions. The quotations also give a good idea of how many good books on preaching are available, and will help readers decide which one(s) to read next.

The book is divided into three sections. The first one lays the basic foundations on which our approach to preaching must rest. It does this by considering preaching as the communication of God's Word (Chapter 1) to groups of people (Chapter 2). The second and longest section deals with the entire preaching process, from when I begin my preparation to when I give my talk (Chapters 3 to 6). The third section is designed to encourage us to make progress in our ability to preach well. It does this by considering the aftermath of giving a talk (Chapter 7) and then reflecting on preaching as a Christian ministry (Chapter 8). With the possible exception of the final one, the chapters of the book need to be read in sequence, because each one builds on what precedes it.

Preaching is not limited to sermons delivered in church. It can be done in many other contexts: in prisons, in lecture theatres in universities and office blocks, in conference centres, in open-air venues such as shopping precincts and so on. That is why this book generally refers to the 'talk' rather than the 'sermon'.

Preaching is not the only right way of communicating God's message to the world, but it is a very important way of doing so – and thus public proclamation of God's Word should be done as widely as possible. This book aims to encourage this vital ministry by showing readers how to do this effectively.

PART 1

PRINCIPLES

1. Preaching and God

1.1. Preaching and God: To get you thinking...

A recent survey from the Bureau of Depressing Religious Statistics says this:

The average churchgoer remembers 0.03 per cent of all sermons heard. After 10 minutes, he (or she these days!) starts thinking about lunch. After 20 minutes, they stop hearing a word you say and start finding the notice sheet interesting. (At least you've worked one miracle.) After 30 minutes, they've forgotten the bit they actually listened to at the beginning. After 40 minutes, they start wondering if it's possible to commit suicide by impaling themselves on their car keys.

How should we respond to such surveys? Burn them. And their compilers where available. It's just ammunition for those who would do down the holy art of the sermon...If they don't feel they're getting much out of your sermons, preach a series on 'Sermons: God's Number One Priority', and hopefully they'll see the error of their ways.

Rev'd Gerald Ambulance, My Ministry Manual, (London: SPCK, 2002), p. 33f.

...to what method of teaching must pastors adhere?...he will teach whatever is revealed in Scripture, although he will do so prudently and opportunely for the upbuilding of the people, yet simply and without any pretence, as befits a faithful and frank interpreter of God... the men who make known the will of God are those who expound Scripture faithfully, and from it establish the people in faith, in the fear of the Lord, and in all godly practices.

John Calvin, Calvin's New Testament Commentaries, 12 volumes (Grand Rapids, 1966 [1552]), 7.180-81 (on Acts 20:27).

The pressure of weekly deadlines, the desire to satisfy people's varying expectations, the distraction of difficult pastoral situations, the discouragement of criticism, and the plethora of ideas promoted regarding contemporary ministry, may combine to distort our view of what preaching is all about. We may find that slowly, subtly our confidence in the authority of the Word wanes, our commitment to preparation diminishes, our convictions about preaching are watered down, and our goals become blurred. If we are to withstand such pressures we need to have a very clear-minded view of what preaching is all about. Without a strong theology of preaching driving our ministry forward we will most likely lose heart and lose focus.

Murray A. Capill, *Preaching with Spiritual Vigour,* (Fearn: Christian Focus, 2003), p. 85f.

One aged person remembered how a rude multitude had been swayed when John Wesley preached in the cattle market; but for a long while it had not been expected of preachers that they should shake the souls of men.

George Eliot, *The Mill on the Floss,* (Glasgow: Collins, 1979 [1860]), p. 119.

We may study the presentation of sermons from the viewpoint of the preacher, or the audience, or the times, or the church, or moral values, or any number of other perspectives. Though each of these vantage points is important, the most basic consideration is the purpose of God for preaching. Unless we understand that, the rest is more or less irrelevant.

Wayne V. McDill, *The Moment of Truth,* (Nashville: Broadman & Holman, 1999), p. 6.

Preaching has become a by-word for a long and dull conversation of any kind; and whoever wishes to imply, in any piece of writing, the absence of everything agreeable and inviting, calls it a sermon.

Rev'd Sydney Smith (1771–1845), quoted in Lady S Holland, *Memoirs,* (1855).

There is, perhaps, no greater hardship at present inflicted on mankind in civilised and free countries, than the necessity of listening to sermons. No one but a preaching clergyman has, in these realms, the power of compelling an audience to sit silent, and be tormented...A member of Parliament can be coughed down or counted out. But no one can rid himself of the preaching clergyman. He is the bore of the age...We desire...to enjoy the comfort of public worship; but we desire also that we may do so without an amount of tedium which ordinary human nature cannot endure with patience; that we may be able to leave the house of God, without that anxious longing for escape, which is the common consequence of common sermons.

Anthony Trollope, *Barchester Towers*, (London: Hamlyn, 1987 [1857]), p. 47.

1.2.   Preaching and God: Guidance from Scripture

...he had compassion on them, because they were like sheep without a shepherd. So he began teaching them many things.

Mark 6:34.

In the presence of God and of Christ Jesus, who will judge the living and the dead, and in view of his appearing and his kingdom, I give you this charge: Proclaim the word...

2 Timothy 4:1-2.

A backpacker on a walking tour of Ireland realized that he was lost. Noticing an old fellow sunning himself on a nearby bench, he went over and asked him, 'Can you please tell me how to get to Cork?' The elderly gent thought about this for a while, and then said, 'If I was you and I wanted to get to Cork, I wouldn't start from here.'

1.3.   Beginning at the beginning

There is obviously a lot to be said for starting at the right place, so where should a guidebook for preachers begin? For obvious reasons, many people would expect to begin with *how* – how to prepare a talk, and how to preach it. After all, what a starving church and a perishing world need most is not theoreticians but practitioners; not people who can discuss preaching, but people who can preach. But *how* is *not* where we should begin and that for two reasons.

The first is that we have not defined what we mean by 'preaching.' It always helps to know what we are talking about! The second and more important reason is that the best preachers – those who not only preach well now, but who go on growing as preachers – are those who possess *know-what* and *know-why* as well as know-how. This should cause no surprises, because in all areas of Christian service *what* and *why* are more important than *how*. Why is this? One reason is that people who have only been taught 'how' are in the proverbial 'up-the-creek-without-a-paddle' dilemma when faced by a situation they have not been trained or equipped for – '*Now* what am I supposed to do?!' The reality is that no amount of training can prepare people in advance for everything they might have to face. So instructors who are content with imparting know-how will leave God's servants badly under-equipped for the challenges and opportunities they will face in their lives and ministries.

Another and more important reason for not putting *how* in charge is that this will only breed pragmatists. Servants of calibre are those whose *practice* is the fruit of deeply-rooted *principle*. But the most important reason of all for keeping *how* in its place is that no discussion of preaching (or any other Christian ministry) should focus primarily on *our* work. First and foremost, we need to understand preaching in connection with God and *his* work. So before we look at how to preach, we need to consider some much more fundamental issues.

The most fundamental issue we need to consider is this: What is God doing in the world? What is his work? Next comes the question of what part his Word plays in that work. And then we can look at the various 'ministries of the Word' that are both the result and also the means of God's speaking. In that context, we can then work out what preaching is and how we should go about it.

These are the issues we would now go on to consider if this book aimed to provide a comprehensive treatment of preaching. However, because it is designed to be a guidebook, I am going to assume that you have already sorted these matters out sufficiently for us to proceed to the next step.[1] But in case that makes you nervous, here is a checklist of the fundamental truths I have in mind:

i.   God's work of progressively revealing his person and purposes

---

[1]   If you are now wondering what you should think about these fundamental issues, you will find a helpful discussion of them in Peter Adam's *Speaking God's Words*, (Leicester: IVP, 1996), especially chapters 1, 4, and 6, and his *Written For Us: Receiving God's Words in the Bible*, (Nottingham: IVP, 2008).

reaches its climax in his Son. As redemption is accomplished in the Son, so revelation too is completed in him – and the supremacy of his person guarantees the sufficiency of his work as both Revealer and Redeemer. Because of who he is, neither of these twin dimensions of his work needs to be supplemented, and neither could be surpassed.[2]

ii. The work of the Son is surrounded and implemented by the work of the Spirit. The Spirit's work is not to add to the work of the Son, but to establish it in our lives – what the Son accomplished, the Spirit applies. So the Spirit prepared for the Son's coming into the world by equipping prophets to speak God's Word, indicating the work the Son was to do. Then, when the Son had returned to the Father's side, the Spirit equipped the apostles to speak God's Word, spelling out what we have in and through the Son.[3]

> Let this be a firm principle: No other word is to be held as the Word of God, and given place as such in the church, than what is contained first in the Law and the Prophets, then in the writings of the apostles; and the only authorized way of teaching in the church is by the...standard of this Word...[This] is the difference between the apostles and their successors: the former were sure and genuine scribes of the Holy Spirit, and their writings are therefore to be considered as oracles of God; but the sole office of others is to teach what is provided and sealed in the Holy Scriptures.[4]

iii. The Spirit secured in written form the revelation that was given through the prophets and apostles, and in the Son to whom they both testified. Because of the Spirit's work, in their words we have God's words. This means that the Bible is God's Word written. In fact, it is not going too far to say that the Bible is God preaching to us.[5]

---

[2] See Luke 24:25-27, 44-47; John 1:1, 14; Colossians 1:15-20; 2:2-15; Hebrews 1:1-4; 2 John 9.

[3] See John 14:26; 16:12-15; 1 Corinthians 2:12-13; 1 Thessalonians 2:13; 4:1-3, 8; 1 Peter 1:10-12; 2 Peter 1:21; 3:2, 16.

[4] John Calvin, *Institutes of the Christian Religion*, 2 volumes, (Library of Christian Classics), (London: SCM, 1961 [1559], IV.viii.8, 9), 2.1155, 1157.

[5] See 2 Samuel 23:2; Jeremiah 36:1-10; Matthew 19:4-5; 22:31-32; John 14:26; 15:26-27; 16:12-15; 1 Corinthians 14:37; Hebrews 3:7-11; 10:15-17; 1 Peter 1:10-12; 2 Peter 1:21; 3:2.

...the sermons or homilies written or spoken by men, are explications and exhortations but of themselves they are not the word of God. In a sermon, the text only is in a proper sense to be called God's word...For God preaches to us in the Scripture; good men preach to us when they...expound and press any of those doctrines which God hath preached unto us in his holy word...the Holy Ghost is certainly the best preacher in the world, and the words of Scripture the best sermons...good sermons and good books are of excellent use; but yet they can serve no other end but that we practise the plain doctrines of Scripture.[6]

iv.   The Spirit now ensures that the message of this public-domain revelation, the Bible as God's Word, is made effective in our lives. We rely on his continuing work of 'illumination' (a subjective – or small 'r' – revelation) to grasp the meaning of the Scriptures (the objective – or big 'R' – Revelation) that were created by his once-for-all work of 'inspiration'.[7]

v.   In every time and place, the contents of the written Word of God need to be translated, interpreted, and applied, so that those who are perishing find life in the Son and those who are being saved grow to fullness of life in him. These necessary ministries are to be carried out in dependence on the powerful work of the Spirit in people, with people, and through people.[8]

vi.   There are many 'ministries of the Word' – many ways in which the Bible's message needs to be lodged in our minds and lives – but one that will always be necessary is the ministry of preaching: that is, declaring, explaining, and applying God's Word to groups of people.[9]

    ...since faith comes by hearing, and hearing by the Word of God...the Church cannot possibly spring up or be built

---

[6]   Jeremy Taylor, *The Rule and Exercises of Holy Living,* (New York: Harper & Row, 1970 [1651]), p. 120.

[7]   See Luke 24:45; Acts 1:16, 20; 4:25-28; 1 Corinthians 2:12-13; Ephesians 1:17-21; 2 Timothy 3:16.

[8]   See Acts 4:18-31; 8:30-35; Ephesians 4:11-13; Colossians 1:28; 3:16; 1 Thessalonians 1:4-5, 9-10; 2 Thessalonians 2:13-15.

[9]   See Acts 6:2-4; Galatians 6:6; 1 Timothy 4:6, 13, 15-16; 2 Timothy 2:1-2, 14-15; 4:1-5; Titus 1:9; Hebrews 13:7; 1 Peter 1:12; 4:10-11a.

by the decrees and doctrines of men. Hence we affirm that only the Word of God is apt for the building up of the Church of God. The doctrines of men set up the churches of men, but Christ's Word builds up the Christian Church...Therefore let us hold that the Church is...founded, planted, assembled and built only by the Word of Christ. We add that the Church is undoubtedly preserved by the same Word of God, lest at any time it should be seduced and should slip and perish, and that it can never be preserved by any other means...having given teachers to the Church our Lord God founds, builds, maintains and enlarges the Church by his Word and his Word alone.[10]

1.4. *What is preaching?*

What is preaching, and how is it distinguished from other 'ministries of the Word'? A simple way of making the answer clear is to construct a 'concept ladder.' This means starting with the most basic and obvious fact about preaching, and then asking a series of questions that enable us to distinguish it from other similar activities. It works like this:

What is preaching?
Preaching is an activity performed by human beings.

Which category of human activity does it belong to?
Preaching is a type of communication.

Which category of human communication does it belong to?
Preaching belongs to that type of communication that is carried out by means of *speaking,* rather than by writing, for example. So preaching differs from the ministry of those who write Christian literature.

---

[10] Heinrich Bullinger, 'Of the Holy Catholic Church' in G. W. Bromiley [ed.], *Zwingli and Bullinger,* (Library of Christian Classics), (Philadelphia: Westminster, 1953), p. 307-9.

What category of spoken communication does it belong to?

Preaching belongs to that form of speaking that is done *publicly*, not privately. It means addressing a group of people, not just one or two individuals. So it differs from evangelistic or pastoral conversations.

What category of public speaking does it belong to?

Preaching belongs to the type of public speaking that is done as a *monologue* rather than a dialogue. So it differs from a public debate or a Bible study group.

What category of monologue does it belong to?

Unlike the monologue that aims primarily to inform (such as a lecture) or to entertain (like a comedy routine), preaching aims to *change* its hearers. It will inform, but it will also invite; it seeks to persuade as well as to proclaim; it will consist of exhortation as well as explanation. So preaching differs from the ministry of the Word carried out by those who give academic lectures.

Why does preaching have this aim?

The basic reason lies in what is being communicated. Because preaching is a vehicle by which God's Word is conveyed to the hearers, its aims are determined by that Word. Preaching has no agenda of its own; it seeks only to have the Spirit of God bring the Word of God into our lives powerfully and effectively.

This quick trip up the concept ladder has explained how 'preaching' is being used in this guidebook. It has a narrower sense than in some circles, where it applies to virtually any way that the Bible's message is communicated. It is also being used more widely than in some other contexts, for its meaning is not being limited to 'giving the sermon in church'. While this will be the kind of preaching most people encounter, preaching can also be done in a variety of other settings.

Our trip up the ladder has made another important fact clear to us: that preaching has two sides to it. As human communication, preaching has much in common with other types of public speaking. Yet because it is a means of communicating God's Word, it differs from other kinds of public speaking in some very fundamental ways. If we are to understand preaching rightly, then, we must look at it from both of these complementary perspectives. The first and most important is the *vertical* perspective, where our focus is on *what* is being communicated. The second is *horizontal,* where our focus is on *how* the message is communicated. The former connects preaching with God's work and Word, the latter looks at it as a way of influencing the lives of the hearers.

Just before we move on, let me give you two simple and effective ways of seeing the fundamental importance of the ministry of preaching. The first is to note the central place this ministry had in the work of:

- Jesus (e.g., Mark 1:37-38; 2:1-2, 13; 4:1; 6:6b, 34; 9:30-31; 10:1; 14:49)

- the twelve apostles (e.g., Acts 2:42; 5:42; 6:1-4; 8:25; 10:40-42)

- Paul (e.g., Acts 28:30-31; 1 Corinthians 1:17; Col 1:23-29; 1 Thessalonians 2:1-13; 2 Thessalonians 3:1; 2 Timothy 1:11)

- Paul's associates, such as Timothy (e.g., 1 Timothy 4:11-16; 2 Timothy 2:2, 14-18, 24-26; 4:1-5)

- local church leaders (e.g., Galatians 6:6; 1 Timothy 3:2; 5:17; 2 Timothy 2:2, 24; 4:1-5; Titus 1:9; Hebrews 13:7).

The second is to analyse Paul's review of his ministry in Ephesus (Acts 20:17-35). Once you have read this passage several times, look for answers to the following questions:

- What was the scope of Paul's ministry? That is, what activities did it include?

- What was its centre or focus?

- What were its methods?

- What was its overall aim?

- Despite the problems he foresaw, what gave Paul confidence about the future?

I hope that you will make time to do both of these case studies, because they will give you a very clear picture of some basic truths about the work and Word of God. It will become especially clear that, having entrusted his very words to us in written form, God wants us to tell others what he says. And he wants those with the necessary gifts to do this on a regular basis, speaking his words to others so that they will come to Christ and grow in Christ.

This leads us to an important conclusion. If preaching is a means of communicating God's Word, and thus a means by which God does his work in people's lives, then it is not an opportunity for me to give my opinions on a subject of my choosing to any group that is willing to give me a hearing. The preacher is a messenger, not an oracle; a herald rather than a lecturer; an announcer, not an author; a deliverer and not a manufacturer. Whatever else it is, preaching should be biblical.

1.5.   *What is expository preaching?*

There are several ways in which preaching can be connected to the Bible, but the one I want to recommend is known as 'expository' preaching. To understand more clearly what that is, let us take a quick look at some other forms of preaching.

One is the kind of preaching which begins by referring to a particular verse or passage in the Bible and then proceeds to ignore it more or less completely. The Bible is used like a launch pad and the talk is like the rocket which leaves the launch pad further behind the longer it stays in the air. Preaching is not biblical when it uses the Bible as nothing more than a way of getting launched. Rather, everything the preacher teaches should be both anchored in the Bible and in accordance with what the Bible teaches.

Does this mean that in order to be biblical, preaching must go through a Bible verse or passage from beginning to end, explaining the meaning word-by-word? No. This is not how we preach; it is how we prepare what we preach. This process of interpretation is called 'exegesis', and we will discover in Chapter 3 that this is how we gather the raw material from which we produce a talk. But it is not what we do in the talk – that would be like inviting guests for a meal, and then making them watch us prepare the meal rather than serving it to them. The desk where I do my preparation is the kitchen bench; the lectern where I do my preaching is the dining table.

What about the kind of preaching which tackles the Bible's big themes, or considers big themes in light of what the Bible as a whole teaches? This might be a talk about 'the faithfulness of God' or 'a biblical view of divorce'. Such talks would not be limited to just one verse or passage in the Bible, but might survey several passages. Isn't this a valid way of doing biblical preaching? My answer is, 'Yes – if you can do it!' The problem with such preaching is that it is very hard to do well, so that only the most gifted preachers can manage to do it in a way that is faithful to the Bible and also helpful to the hearers. The best way the rest of us can tackle an important topic is to base the talk on the Bible passage which has the most to say about it.

This brings us to 'expository' preaching. This has not always had a good reputation. However, the problem does not lie with expository preaching itself but with those who do it poorly. Consider the following example:

> The text for my sermon this morning is the first verse of the thirteenth chapter of the second book of Kings: 'In the twenty-third year of Joash son of Ahaziah king of Judah, Jehoahaz son of Jehu began to reign over Israel in Samaria, and he reigned seventeen years.'

> 'He reigned seventeen years.' There is a treasure trove of meaning here for anyone who is prepared to dig and delve for it, is there not? Only four simple words – but consider what they meant for Jehoahaz. First, of course, came his training for reigning; secondly, in the fullness of time, his gaining of the reigning; next, the maintaining of his reigning; then, the waning of his reigning; and finally, sadly, his refraining from reigning.

> Each of these points can be pondered with profit by the patient and persistent. Which of us, for example, could abstain from complaining during our training for reigning? Or who could sustain the pain of a waning reign?...and so on...and on!

No one would want to sit through such preaching every week – and no one should have to! So if this is not expository preaching, what is? A useful way of beginning our answer to the question is to say what expository preaching isn't and to point out how it differs from other kinds of preaching.

First of all, expository preaching avoids imposing my thoughts and ideas, my aims and agendas, on some part of the Bible. In expository preaching the Bible is in control, and my job is to 'expose' what is contained in the passage concerned. As the similarity with such words as 'exposé' and 'exposure' suggests, this means that I am to uncover what is there, to open up the passage and display its message, to make its meaning clear.

Expository preaching must also be distinguished from what is sometimes called 'topical' preaching. This is the kind of preaching in which I have a topic I want to speak about; I find a Bible verse or passage to fit this topic; my talk uses this part of the Bible as my 'launch pad' into the topic; and my talk says what *I* want to say about the topic. The 'sermon notes' you have just read provide a good example! The important point here is that preaching from a Bible passage does not make preaching 'expository'. A talk on reigning based on 2 Kings 13:1 is not expository preaching because 'reigning' is not the subject of 2 Kings 13:1. The same would apply to a talk against dieting based on Proverbs 13:25, or to an attack on shopping based on Matthew 6:28-31!

Preaching is expository when it is controlled by the Bible and not by the preacher. This applies first of all to the *content* of the talk. In their preparation, expository preachers ask '*what* does this passage teach?' In their preaching, they communicate *the message of the passage*.

Secondly, this applies to the *style* and *structure* of the talk. In their preparation, expository preachers ask '*how* does this passage teach what it teaches?' In their preaching, they seek to communicate the message of the passage *in the way the passage communicates it*.

Thirdly, this applies to the *aim* of the talk. In their preparation, expository preachers ask '*why* does this passage teach what it teaches?' In their preaching, they communicate the message of the passage *in a way that aims at the same response that the passage is aiming at*.

Here is what some experienced preachers have said about expository preaching:

> ...preaching is truly biblical when (a) the Bible governs the content of the sermon and when (b) the function of the sermon is analogous to that of the text. In other words, preaching is biblical when it imparts a Bible-shaped word in a Bible-like way.[11]

Expository preaching is that method of proclaiming the Word of God in which both the *shape* and the *content* of the message

---

11   Leander E. Keck, *The Bible in the Pulpit*, (Nashville: Abingdon, 1978), p. 106.

arise from the passage itself.[12]

> Exposition of Scripture...is that process whereby the meaning of a particular passage in the Bible is so explained in terms of the needs and circumstances of the congregation, that the people understand what God is saying to them.[13]

> Expository preaching consists in the explanation and application of a passage of Scripture. Without explanation it is not expository; without application it is not preaching.[14]

> To expound Scripture is to bring out of the text what is there and expose it to view...The opposite of exposition is 'imposition', which is to impose on the text what is not there...our responsibility as expositors is to open [the text] up in such a way that it speaks its message clearly, plainly, accurately, relevantly, without addition, subtraction, or falsification.[15]

One of the great benefits of expository preaching, and thus one of the best incentives to keep at it, is that it sends the hearers back to their Bibles with a keen sense of how much God has to say to us.

What effect has all this had on you? Are you reeling a bit, because expository preaching now seems to be much bigger than you first thought, and because it seems like really hard work? I hope that is true, for both of these responses are right. Let us take them one at a time, to think a bit more about what expository preaching means.

Expository preaching is not just a matter of my talk being about the same subject as the Bible passage I am using. This is necessary, and without it we do not have expository preaching. But it is not sufficient on its own – to be expository, it is not only the subject of my talk but also its style and shape and direction that must be controlled by the passage. Let us examine the third of these a bit more closely. (We will work on the first and second of them when we get to Chapters 3 and 4.)

Expository preaching must always have a *clear aim*. There are two reasons why this is necessary. The first is that the Bible is a

---

[12]   Walter C. Kaiser in Richard A. Bodey [ed.], *Inside the Sermon*, (Grand Rapids: Baker, 1990), p. 173.
[13]   Denis Lane, *Preach the Word*, (Welwyn: Evangelical, 1979), p. 12.
[14]   T. H. L. Parker, *Calvin's Preaching*, (Louisville: WJK, 1992), p. 79.
[15]   John R. W. Stott, *I Believe in Preaching*, (London: Hodder, 1982), p. 125-6.

purposeful book – God has given us his Word in order to do his work.[16] It is therefore essential that our use of the Bible conforms to God's purposes in giving it to us. What this means in practice is that we must always ask – and when we are preaching, must always answer – two questions about any passage of Scripture. The first is *what*? That is, what does this passage *mean*? The second is *so what*? That is, why do these truths *matter*? This double question reflects a basic pattern in the Bible's teaching: namely, the combination of information and invitation, announcement and appeal, explanation and exhortation. (We see a very clear example of this in Matthew 4:17 and Mark 1:15.) Preaching that is faithfully biblical cannot be restricted only to the first item in these pairs. This is perhaps the major difference between preaching and lecturing. The second reason for having a clear aim is that this is essential for effective communication, something we will investigate in the next chapter.

What will purposeful preaching involve? The aim of any piece of expository preaching will be determined by the aim of the passage it is expounding. I am not doing expository preaching if the aim of every Bible talk I give is to promote evangelism! This is not because evangelism isn't very important, but because it is not the case that most Bible passages are intended to emphasize and encourage evangelism. Then how will my preaching reflect the aim of the passage I am expounding?

i.   I will want my hearers to *receive* God's message – what he is saying in the passage concerned. As far as I am able, I want to ensure that the hearers can *take it in* because of the way my talk *explains* it. This is where the role of the preacher overlaps with that of the teacher.

ii.   I will want the hearers to *respond* to God's message. I want to ensure that they can *live it out* because of the way my talk *applies* it. Preaching that conveys the message of the Bible faithfully will therefore involve exhortation as well as explanation. This is where the preacher is like a barrister, 'preaching for a verdict'.

---

[16]   See, for example, Isaiah 55:10-11; Romans 15:4; 1 Corinthians 10:11; 2 Timothy 3:14-17.

If there is no summons, there is no sermon.[17]

...unless we have made a sensitive, compassionate, forceful, and unmistakable application, we have merely done exposition, not expository preaching. We must constantly be asking ourselves not only what we are preaching, but why.[18]

Some preachers presume that their task is merely to proclaim the gospel, to speak the truth, to herald the good news...This view of preaching...assumes that if people know the truth, they will respond to it; the preacher's role is to tell them the truth. But in reality, people often have to be encouraged to act upon what they know to be true. Preaching persuades hearers to act upon the revelation of God.[19]

iii.   Although this is not directly related to the aim of the passage, I will also want the hearers to *remember* God's message. I will want to ensure that they can *'play it back'* because of the way my talk *presents* it.

This is a very important, but often neglected, aspect of my role as a preacher. What is the point of working hard for ten or twelve hours to prepare a talk that lasts for twenty-five or thirty minutes and then disappears forever? Why should God's message be limited to half an hour, so that it is absent from the remaining one hundred-and-sixty-seven-and-a-half hours in the hearers' week? Shouldn't I want my hearers to recall the message of the passage during the week, so that it can go on doing its work in their lives? Surely our motto as preachers should be, *If it is worth saying, it is worth remembering!* And that means that we have to work hard at crafting our Bible talks in a way that makes it as easy as possible for the hearers to remember the message and so to keep on appropriating it and responding to it. (More of this in Chapters 4 and 5, when we look at preparing talks.)

---

[17] John A. Broadus, *On the Preparation and Delivery of Sermons*, (new & revised edition by Jesse Burton Weatherspoon), (Nashville: Broadman, 1944), p. 210.

[18] Walter L. Liefeld, *New Testament Exposition*, (Grand Rapids: Zondervan, 1984), p. 107.

[19] Craig Loscalzo, *Preaching Sermons that Connect*, (Downers Grove: IVP, 1992), p. 18.

> [Jesus] employed forms and techniques of speech that
> enabled his hearers to remember what he said...Jesus
> consciously formulated his preaching and teaching to make
> it memorisable.[20]

> The sermon-outline is a set of shelves upon which the main
> thoughts can be arranged in the listener's mind. It becomes
> a basket in which he can carry most of the material home. It
> may even become a pocket book from which, at work in the
> middle of the week, he can extract the remnants of what he
> heard, and be blessed again.[21]

So purposeful preaching, expository preaching that takes its aim from
the intention of the passage being expounded, will seek to enable the
hearers to take the message in and to live the message out (and also to
play the message back).

And this brings us to your second reaction, that expository
preaching seems like really hard work. You are quite right about this, and
that is why expository preaching is much rarer than it should be. After
preachers have had some preaching experience, they find that topical
preaching doesn't take much time to prepare and so isn't too demanding.
But expository preaching usually requires lots of time and is almost
always hard work. This means that preachers will not remain committed
to expository preaching throughout the whole of their ministries unless
they are fully convinced (i) that the Bible is God's Word, that is, God
speaking or preaching to us, and (ii) that God uses his Word to do his
work in people's lives. Do you see what this means? It takes us right back
to where we began, for this is one very obvious way in which *know-what*
and *know-why* prove to be more important and more powerful than *know-how*. What I do in my preaching will depend on what I believe about the
Word of God, and on what I believe about the God of the Word.

> ...we must have [the] confidence that it is the word of God, in the
> hands of the Spirit of God, that does the work of God.[22]

---

[20]   C. Richard Wells and A. Boyd Luter, *Inspired Preaching*, (Nashville: Broadman &
       Holman, 2002), p. 176.
[21]   R. E. O. White, *A Guide to Preaching*, (London: Pickering & Inglis, 1973), p. 82.
[22]   David Jackman in William Philip [ed.], *The Practical Preacher*, (Fearn: Christian
       Focus, 2002), p. 31f.

In a world which seems either unwilling or unable to listen, how can we be persuaded to go on preaching, and learn to do so effectively? The essential secret is not mastering certain techniques but being mastered by certain convictions. In other words, theology is more important than methodology...there are principles of preaching to be learned, and a practice to be developed, but it is easy to put too much confidence in these. Technique can only make us orators; if we want to be preachers, theology is what we need.[23]

1.6. How do expositors preach?

There is another side to this particular coin; while expository preaching requires hard work, it also brings great freedom. In contrast to the topical preacher, the expository preacher deals with issues as and when the Bible itself raises them. When I am preaching through one of the New Testament letters, I am bound to deal with the whole range of subjects: sexual sin, marriage and divorce, greed, disputes and church splits, suffering and death, family life, and a great many others, that the letter tackles. I cannot be accused of choosing to speak on such matters in order to have a go at someone, or to ride one of my hobbyhorses.

The second way in which I am free is that God stands behind his Word and uses it to do his work. As an expository preacher, I am a messenger and not a salesman. I am responsible to deliver the message as faithfully and effectively as I can, but I am not responsible for the outcome; I do not have to produce or guarantee results. Paul made the point this way: 'I planted the seed, Apollos watered it, but God has been making it grow.' (1 Corinthians 3:6). The preacher will always feel stretched, for the challenge of doing the best we can do will never go away. But the preacher should never feel crushed, for the terrible burden of needing to succeed is not one we should bear. I can confidently leave the outcome of my preaching in God's hands.

Expository preaching...requires discipline and diligence but it also brings freedom. Freedom is found in realizing that effectiveness and power in preaching are not dependent on

---

[23]   John R. W. Stott, *I Believe in Preaching*, p. 92.

being clever, witty and smart...If the message preached is full of the Word, and opens faithfully the message of Scripture, we may be sure that it will not return to the Lord void.[24]

Let us persevere with our task and leave the success to the Lord...Such is the power of the Word of God that to effect nothing and to profit no one is impossible.[25]

I hope you will always feel your responsibility before God; but do not carry the feeling too far. We may feel our responsibility so deeply that we become unable to sustain it; it may cripple our joy, and make slaves of us. Do not take an exaggerated view of what the Lord expects of you. He will not blame you for not doing that which is beyond your mental power or physical strength. You are required to be faithful, but you are not bound to be successful. You are to teach, but you cannot compel people to learn. You are to make things plain, but you cannot give carnal men an understanding of spiritual things. We are not the Father, nor the Saviour, nor the Comforter of the Church.[26]

What does this mean in practice? How does the freedom of being a messenger rather than a salesman, being confident not in my preaching abilities but in the power of God's Word to do God's work, show itself in my preaching?

Perhaps the most obvious characteristic of expository preaching will be its faithfulness. Preachers who see themselves as salesmen with a product to sell will always be tempted to change the message to make it more marketable. This is exactly what happened in Paul's day – some preachers manipulated the message to make it more likely to fill their pay packets and collection bowls (2 Corinthians 2:17; 4:1-2). In contrast to them, Paul and his colleagues refused to modify the message to make it more palatable. They knew it was not theirs – they had been entrusted with God's Word, and had no right to tamper with it. And they knew that the undiluted Word of God would, by the working of the Spirit of God, do the work of God, even when the hearers were opposed to it (1

---

[24]   Murray A. Capill, *Preaching with Spiritual Vigour*, p. 93.

[25]   John Jewel, *Works*, 4 volumes, (The Parker Society), (Cambridge: CUP, 1847), iii.955 (ca. 1551; language modernized).

[26]   Charles H. Spurgeon, *An All-Round Ministry*, (Edinburgh: Banner of Truth, 1960 [1900]), p. 214.

Corinthians 1:18, 22-24). As a result, they remained faithful in the face of many pressures to compromise; they set forth God's truth plainly (2 Corinthians 4:2).

Along with this faithfulness to the message, expository preaching will also be marked by earnestness. Since it is God's message that I am communicating, I will mean business in my preaching. I will want my hearers to understand and receive and respond to the message, to take it in and live it out. I will work hard at crafting my talk with this aim in view; I will be praying that God will bring this about; I will speak in a way that encourages this outcome.

> For effectiveness in delivery nothing takes the place of deep sincerity and strong conviction. The preacher who preaches with conviction speaks from his heart and there is power in such preaching. If he believes earnestly in what he is saying and is convinced that it has great importance for his hearers and that they should be persuaded by the truth which he is speaking, a man will speak with fervor and power. All the technical knowledge and training in the art of speech which a man can acquire will not take the place of this sense of conviction and responsibility.[27]

> Hearing the word of God read and preached ought to be an experience which engages the whole personality. It is tragic to hear sermons on...the seriousness of sin, the majesty of Jesus, the assurance of salvation, the expectation of glory, delivered with all the passion one might show in giving street directions to a passing motorist.[28]

And yet I will not preach like a driven person. Because I want the message to do its work in the hearers' lives, I will be earnest – but because I trust God to use his Word to do his work, I will also be calm. My earnestness will not be drivenness, because I trust God about the outcome. And my calmness will not be carelessness either, because I know this matters enormously. So when preaching is expository it will combine two characteristics that seem like opposites.

Another pair of apparent opposites that are combined in

---

[27]   Bob Jones, Jr., *How to Improve Your Preaching*, (Old Tappan, NJ: Revell, 1945), p. 74.
[28]   Mike Raiter, *Stirrings of the Soul*, (Kingsford: Matthias Media, 2003), p. 248.

expository preaching is authority and humility. Because I am communicating God's message, I will speak with authority and, because I too must take that message to heart and live it out in my life, I will speak with humility. Expository preachers are not authoritarian; we are to be bold but not cold or heartless. But nor are we to be spineless. There must be courage but also compassion, gentleness but also grittiness. Because it is God's Word, what we are preaching must be heard and heeded, accepted and obeyed and, because it is God's Word, we should be the very first who respond to it in this way.

> Pastoral authority can be attained only by the servant of Jesus who seeks no power of his own, who himself is a brother among brothers submitted to the authority of the Word.[29]

> ...the more the preacher has 'trembled' at God's Word himself, and felt its authority upon his conscience and in his life, the more he will be able to preach it with authority to others.[30]

There are two final things that must never not be said and yet they seem so obvious that it is amazingly easy to take them for granted and leave them out. I am referring, first, to the fact that faithful preaching of God's Word will always be centred upon the person of God's Son, because he is the true centre and subject of the entire Bible. (Note the three uses of 'all' in Luke 24:25-27 and see also Luke 24:44-46; John 5:39-40, 46; 2 Corinthians 1:20). To preach God's Word is to preach God's Son in all his glory as Lord and all his grace as Saviour.

> [The preacher] must have a zeal for Christ, and must aim at nothing so much as to bring sinners to him. This should be in some measure the design and drift of every sermon that he preaches...For this should every minister study and strive, and for this should he continually pray that God would fill his heart with pious zeal and holy wisdom, so that he may divide the word of truth aright, and minister grace to his hearers.[31]

> ...preach *Christ*, always and evermore. He is the whole gospel.

---

[29]   Dietrich Bonhoeffer, *Life Together*, (London: SCM, 1954), p. 85.
[30]   John R. W. Stott, *The Preacher's Portrait*, (London: Tyndale, 1961), p. 26.
[31]   August H. Francke, A Letter to a Friend Concerning the Most Useful Way of Preaching, in Peter C. Erb [ed.], *Pietists: Selected Writings*, (The Classics of Western Spirituality), (London: SPCK, 1983 [1725]), p. 120f.

His person, offices, and work must be our one great, all-comprehending theme.[32]

Preaching Christ means much more than merely mentioning his name occasionally in the sermon...[It] means proclaiming the Word of God in such a way that Jesus Christ is clearly presented in all the fullness of his person and the greatness of his work...He is magnified as the heart of every Christian doctrine and the motivation for every Christian duty.[33]

The second thing that must not be left out is that every aspect of our preaching should be accompanied by prayer. It is simply perverse and ungodly to set myself to speak God's Word without relying upon God's work. I cannot truly do for God what I do without God.

1.7. *Can preaching be learned?*

This is a question that must be faced before we go any further. Is there really any point in a guidebook for preachers? Can people be trained to preach? Surely preachers are born and not made! This is an important issue, for the answer will have a big impact on what I expect of myself and other Christians. So what is the answer?

Are people born with the gift of preaching? I do not believe so. But what some people are born with is what is known in my part of the world as the 'gift of the gab'. That is, they find public speaking relatively easy. I am one of these people. My father claims that I came out of the womb talking, and that when my mother took me to the infant health clinic for my first inoculation, the nurse accidentally injected me with a gramophone needle! In secondary school I joined the debating team, and found that I could string words together fairly easily. Because others noticed this, I was encouraged to become a lay preacher at the age of seventeen, when I had only been a Christian for three years. I didn't know enough then to say 'No', but I doubt that the result was all that helpful, either to my hearers or to me. One of many mistakes I made was that I relied on my way with words, on my ability to rise to the

---

[32]   Charles H. Spurgeon, *Lectures to My Students,* (Grand Rapids: Zondervan, 1954 [1881]), p. 341.

[33]   Warren W. Wiersbe, *The Dynamics of Preaching,* (Grand Rapids: Baker, 1999), p. 31-32.

occasion. This meant that I had many errors to unlearn and many new ways to learn when I became a pastor. My gift with words was a trap – but when it was disciplined and harnessed in the right ways, it could also be a real benefit.

> ...watch your strength. Not so much your weaknesses: it is your strength you have to watch, the things at which you excel, your natural gifts and aptitudes. They are the ones that are most likely to trip you because they are the ones that will tempt you to make a display and to pander to self.[34]

Perhaps your story is a bit like mine. If so, you need to recognize that your ease with public speaking is a potential pitfall, but also a gift that can be used effectively in preaching.

> Even the most gifted preachers weren't born that way. Rather, they have added to their natural gifts and desire a disciplined approach to their craft resulting in consistently meaningful and effective preaching.[35]

But perhaps your story is very different from mine. You find public speaking an ordeal, and would prefer to sit in the audience than stand up front. Yet you too can learn to preach effectively, for learning to preach is quite like learning to play a musical instrument. As a beginner, even if I have an innate musical talent, I have to work hard at learning the right techniques for playing the instrument. Mastering them only comes through lots of practice. By doing the hard work that is necessary I will reach the point where I can concentrate on *what* I am playing (the piece of music) instead of *how* I am playing the instrument. My freedom to play expressively rather than mechanically is the reward for all my hard work. The same goes for my ability to preach effectively – it will come through a disciplined attention to the basic principles and through lots of practice.

So the question is not whether I can speak confidently now, but whether I am willing to have a go and whether I am determined to speak God's words as clearly and faithfully as I can. If this is where you are, you can read on, expecting to learn how to become an effective preacher. God is not dependent on superstars; he uses the willing. It is

---

[34] Martyn Lloyd-Jones, *Preaching and Preachers*, (London: Hodder & Stoughton, 1971), p. 255.
[35] Thomas R. Swears, *Preaching to Head and Heart*, (Nashville: Abingdon, 2000), p. 86.

true, however, that not everyone should serve by standing up the front – just as not everyone can play a musical instrument, however hard they work at it. There are many other ways of serving, and all of them matter to God (1 Corinthians 12:4-6; 1 Peter 4:10-11). So if you really can't see that there is any point in trying to turn yourself into a preacher and, more importantly, if nobody else can either, then you might pass this book on to someone who should be using it.

GOT IT?

i.   Why are 'know-what' and 'know-why' more important than 'know-how'?

ii.   What is 'preaching'?

iii. What is 'expository' preaching? How does it differ from 'topical' preaching?

iv.   What three aims will an expository preacher have?

v.   What are the characteristic marks of the expository preacher?

vi.   In what ways can preaching be learned?

2. Preaching to People

2.1. Preaching to People: To get you thinking...

If I should enter the pulpit without deigning to glance at a book, and frivolously imagine to myself, 'Oh well, when I preach, God will give me enough to say,' and come here without troubling to read, or thinking what I ought to declare, and do not carefully consider how I must apply Holy Scripture to the edification of the people – then I should be an arrogant upstart!

John Calvin, quoted in T. H. L. Parker, *The Oracles of God: An Introduction to the Preaching of John Calvin*, (London: Lutterworth, 1947), p. 69.

'I smell a Lollard in the wind!' said he.
'Good men,' our Host went on, 'attend to me;
Don't run away! By Jesu's noble passion,
We're in for something done in sermon-fashion.
This Lollard here would like to preach, that's what.'
The Skipper said, 'By thunder, he shall not!
He shan't come here to vex us with his preaching,
His commentaries and his Gospel-teaching.
We all believe in God round here,' said he...

Geoffrey Chaucer, *The Canterbury Tales,* rev'd ed., (Penguin Classics), (Harmondsworth: Penguin, 1960 [1386-1400]), p. 173.

Mr Cleves has the wonderful art of preaching sermons which the wheelwright and the blacksmith can understand, not because he talks condescending twaddle, but because he can call a spade a spade, and knows how to disencumber ideas of their wordy frippery.

George Eliot, 'The Sad Fortunes of the Reverend Amos Barton' in *Scenes of Clerical Life,* (Wordsworth Classics), (Ware: Wordsworth, 2007 [1858]), p. 47f.

...he preached such a sermon as never was heard by human ears, at least never by ears of Auchtermuchty. It was a true, sterling, gospel sermon – it was striking, sublime, and awful in the extreme...He proved all the people in [the town], to their perfect satisfaction, to be in the gall of bitterness and the bond of iniquity, and he assured them that God would overturn them...The good people of Auchtermuchty were in perfect raptures with the preacher, who had thus sent them to Hell...Nothing in the world delights a truly religious people so much as consigning them to eternal damnation.

James Hogg, The Private Memoirs and Confessions of a Justified Sinner, (Wordsworth Classics), (Ware: Wordsworth, 2003 [1824]), p. 138.

The minister gave out his text and droned along monotonously through an argument that was so prosy that many a head by-and-by began to nod...It was a genuine relief to the whole congregation when the ordeal was over and the benediction pronounced.

Mark Twain, The Adventures of Tom Sawyer, (Penguin Classics), (London: Penguin, 1986 [1876]), pp. 37, 39.

Question 159: How is the word of God to be preached by those that are called thereunto?

Answer: They that are called to labour in the ministry of the word are to preach sound doctrine, diligently, in season and out of season; plainly, not in the enticing words of man's wisdom, but in demonstration of the Spirit, and of power; faithfully, making known the whole counsel of God; wisely, applying themselves to the necessities and capacities of the hearers; zealously, with fervent love to God and the souls of his people; sincerely, aiming at his glory, and their conversion, edification, and salvation.

The Westminster Larger Catechism (1648).

2.2. Preaching to People: Guidance from Scripture

You know that I have not hesitated to preach anything that would be helpful to you but have taught you publicly and from house to house.

Acts 20:20.

...be prepared in season and out of season; correct, rebuke and encourage – with great patience and careful instruction.

2 Timothy 4:2.

On the way home from church, the nine-year-old announced that he was going to be a preacher when he grew up. 'What made you decide that?' asked his mother. He replied, 'You'll make me go to church anyway, and it is much more fun to stand up and shout than to sit still and listen.' Let's hope that he changed his mind, not necessarily about being a preacher, but about what preaching is. As we saw in the last chapter, it is an exercise in communication. Hence the rather odd title of this chapter, which probably seems so obvious that you were wondering why the publisher didn't jazz it up a bit! But it's there to remind us of the second most important fact about preaching.

The most important is what we were looking at in the last chapter, the fact that preaching communicates God's Word. That was looking at preaching from a *vertical* perspective, that is, as an instrument of God's work in the world. Having considered the *What?* of preaching, now we come to the *Where?* We are shifting our focus from what our preaching conveys to where it is directed. We are going to look at preaching from a *horizontal* perspective, that is, as an exercise in human communication.

The main point of the chapter is this: while we must ensure that our preaching is true communication *of* God's words, we must also ensure that it is real communication *with* our hearers. From this angle, we can think of preaching as bridge building.

2.3. Preaching as bridge building

Good expository preaching builds a bridge between the Bible and the hearers, between God's Word and our world: it connects *text* and *context*.

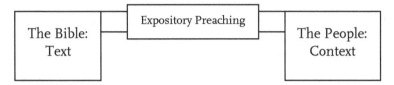

Bridges that stay up rather than collapsing have strong foundations at both ends. This means that expository preachers have to work hard on both the text and the context. We must understand the Bible's message and we must understand our hearers; we must interpret both the Bible and the people accurately.

> ...you must know the One from whom the message comes, you must know the message, and you must know the ones to whom the message will go.[1]

One of the most common mistakes expository preachers make is to put all of their effort into securing just one end of the bridge. It is very easy for us to spend all our preparation time on the *content* of our talks and none on their *context*. We work hard at getting the Bible content right, but spend little or no time on the need to make contact with the hearers. The result is that our talks that are all declaration and little or no exhortation, good in explanation but weak in application. The Bible's message might well be stated accurately and clearly from the lectern, but it might not arrive where the hearers are, or even land anywhere in particular.

> One of the greatest dangers in all public utterance is the bland assumption that truth shared means truth communicated. We all too easily equate telling with teaching, and listening with learning...[2]

Because this is so important we will re-visit one of the case studies from the last chapter. This is where we analysed Paul's review of his ministry in Ephesus (Acts 20:17-35), to see what we could learn about his 'ministry of the Word'. Read through this passage again, this time asking the question, 'What did Paul do in Ephesus?' What answer do you get when you concentrate on the *verbs*?

---

[1]   Graham Johnston, *Preaching to a Postmodern World*, (Grand Rapids: Baker, 2001), p. 64.
[2]   Craig Skinner, *The Teaching Ministry of the Pulpit*, (Grand Rapids: Baker, 1973), p. 93.

This does not give us a complete picture of his ministry, does it? We also need to look at the *nouns* he attaches to the verbs. So he didn't just 'preach' (verse 25), he preached 'the kingdom'; he didn't just 'proclaim' (verse 27), he proclaimed 'the whole will of God'. The verbs tell us the activities Paul engaged in; the nouns tell us the content of those activities. We have to make sure that we get this right, by taking proper note of the nouns as well as the verbs.

> We must be absolutely committed to teaching and preaching the Bible, but to describe our ministry as 'teaching and preaching the Bible' is to describe it in terms of its means, not its end. The purpose of our teaching and preaching the Bible is to explain and commend the good news of God, the gospel of God, the gospel of God's grace, the kingdom of God and the Lord Jesus Christ.[3]

There is one more feature of Paul's report that we must take into account, the *pronouns*. He didn't just proclaim the whole will of God (verse 27); he says, 'I have not hesitated to proclaim *to you* the whole will of God'. He didn't just warn night and day (verse 31); he says, 'I never stopped warning *each of you* night and day'.

Do you see the point? Paul's ministry of the Word was not just speaking general truths into the air. He was not content to declare the truth; he was intent upon connecting the truth with his hearers so that it had its rightful impact in their lives. Paul's example shows us that our understanding of preaching should have a *double focus:* it must centre on both *content* (the What?) and *context* or *contact* (the Where? or the Who to?)

> Books dispense information, but human beings communicate... If all you want to do is impart information, you might as well be a book![4]

Preaching does not mean getting something off our chests or riding our hobbyhorses, having our say because we like to be heard. We are conveying God's message and we are doing so not to everyone in general but to particular groups of people on specific occasions. We preachers are meant to be communicators.

---

[3]   Peter Adam, *Speaking God's Words*, p. 89.
[4]   Hershael W. York & Bert Decker, *Preaching with BOLD Assurance*, (Nashville: Broadman & Holman, 2003), p. 252.

2.4. *Preaching as communicating*

It is absolutely essential that *what* I communicate is *what the Bible teaches*; my preaching must be a communication *of* God's Word. Could there be any greater arrogance, or any greater cruelty to the lost, than to substitute my words for God's? Because God has given us his words, preachers are *heralds* entrusted with a proclamation and *stewards* with a 'deposit' to guard and pass on intact.[5]

This has two implications that are worth pointing out quickly. In the first place, my preaching should be leading the hearers into the Bible all the time, showing them where the text teaches what I am telling them. I want them to be hearing what God is saying, not just what I am saying – and I want them to be able to see that this is what is happening in my talks. Secondly, I should preach in a way that gives the Bible to people rather than taking it from them. If I do my job as a preacher properly, the hearers should be thinking, 'If I had read this passage as carefully and as often as he has done, I could have discovered those truths in it.' They should *not* be left thinking, 'Wow! How does he *do* that?!'

So preaching is communication *of* God's Word, but this is not the whole story. As we learned from Paul's pronouns, it is also essential that I communicate the Bible's message *to my hearers*; my preaching must be communication *with* people. I must be speaking *to* them, not just *at* them. If there is no connection, then there is no communication. As communication, preaching requires *contact* as well as *content*. So I should not be asking, 'How do I get a talk from this text?'

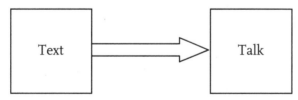

Instead I should be asking, 'How do I get the Bible to the hearers?' My aim is not to capture the teaching of a Bible passage on a piece of paper, but to convey that teaching to a group of people.

---

[5]   John Stott has made a helpful study of these important biblical concepts in *The Preacher's Portrait*.

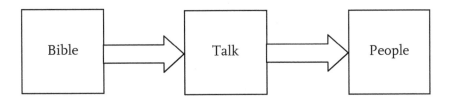

We preachers need to keep on reminding ourselves that preaching is about communicating, conveying God's Word to God's people, speaking God's Word into God's world. Our task is not only about *content*, it is also about *contact* – about making sure that the message is not only said but also heard, not only sent but also received.

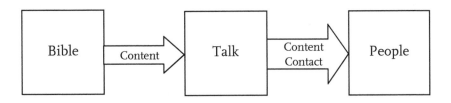

There are two important implications that arise out of what we have just been saying. The first concerns a way of speaking that is very common where I come from. This is the tendency to call preaching, 'teaching the Bible'. There is a good reason for talking like this, but it also involves a danger. Consider the following (completely imaginary!) conversation:

> Chapple: 'What will you do when you have finished your theological training?'
>
> Student: 'I'll be going as a missionary to Tanzania, to teach the Bible.'
>
> Chapple: *(thinks)* 'And what do you think the Bible could learn from you?!'
> *(says,* smiling sweetly) 'Great!'

Do you see the point? To describe preaching as 'Bible teaching' is telling only half the truth. It deals only with the *What?* and ignores the *Where?* But unless I recognize that preaching is also *'people* teaching', my focus is too easily limited to interpreting passages and writing talks, that is, to *content* and not to *contact*.

After preaching a trial sermon to many congregations but never receiving a call to be their pastor, a frustrated young man asked an experienced pastor for help. He was asked to preach one of his sermons to the pastor in private. After he had finished, the pastor said, 'Your problem is simple: you are much more interested in your topic than you are in me.'

[*Other ancient manuscripts read:* After he had finished, the pastor said, 'Your problem is simple: you have spent the last 20 minutes trying to get something out of your head instead of getting something into mine.']

This brings us to the second implication in what we have been saying. Perhaps you are beginning to feel uneasy about all this talk of contact as well as content. If we say that preaching is about making contact, about communication with the hearers, aren't we making ourselves responsible for its impact? And isn't this just another way of saying that we are, after all, responsible for the outcome, so that this isn't only up to God? Perhaps the best way of answering this important question is to recognize that communication has four components: SMCR. The Sender, the Message, the Channel, and the Receiver.

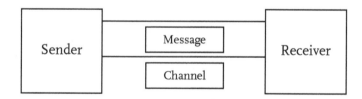

Our concern here is with the third and fourth of these. In the communication we call preaching, the Channel is my talk and the Receiver is the hearer. It is quite true that I have no control over the actual responses of my hearers to what I say, but I do have a good deal of control over their possible responses. This is because I am in control of the Channel by which the Message is being sent. How the Receivers respond to the Message, or whether they can respond to it at all, will be heavily influenced by the way that I send it. At one level, of course, this is very obvious. There is no point giving a talk in English to people who understand only French, or in any spoken language to people who are deaf. At another level, it makes little sense to address a group of six-year-olds as though they were university students, or to lecture about differential calculus to people who lack even a basic grasp of mathematics. So on the one hand, I cannot guarantee the right response, or even any response, to the best talk that I can give. In this sense, the outcome of my preaching really is up to God. But on the other hand, what I say and how I say it will have a big influence on whether the message is understood and received. In this sense, I do have a real responsibility for the outcome of my preaching. There is still great freedom here, because I do not have to be successful, that is, I do not have to secure the right outcomes when I preach. However, as always, I do have to be faithful and here this means working as hard as I can to see that the Bible's message is conveyed in a way that enables it to be understood clearly and appropriated rightly. When I am preparing my talks, I should make it my ambition to be like the wise teacher: 'The Teacher searched to find just the right words, and what he wrote was upright and true.' (Ecclesiastes 12:10).

> If I expect a listener to identify with what I'm saying should I not spend a little time identifying with the listener in the creation of that material? Empathetic imagination![6]

So how do I do this? How can I ensure that I communicate in my preaching?

2.5. *Making contact...by being relevant*

I have been insisting that communicating effectively in preaching involves *making contact* with the hearers. But what does this mean? How can I 'make contact'? The first and most obvious characteristic of preaching that makes effective contact with the hearers' lives will be that it is *relevant*, won't it?

The answer to this question depends entirely on what we think 'relevance' means. If we define relevance as 'telling people what they want to hear', the Bible has a few warning-shots to fire across our bow! But if we define it as 'showing people how the Bible's teaching applies to our lives', then the Bible will encourage us mightily in this endeavour. How does this happen? How do we make our preaching relevant? We do not do so by giving priority to the *context*. If we try to do

---

[6]   Fred Craddock, quoted in John Bodycomb, *Excited to Speak, Exciting to Hear,* (Adelaide: Openbook, 2003), p. 53.

this by attempting to meet people's felt needs, there are some significant difficulties in our path:

- The itches we try to scratch might prove to be merely symptoms and so our preaching would leave the disease untouched. But the Bible aims to *cure* us, not just to comfort us. As a result, it might not connect with our felt needs because it is going to work on needs we do not realize that we have.

- The questions posed by our context might turn out to be irrelevant! The Bible often *changes* our questions, instead of answering them.

- In any audience, there are more needs than a dozen Bible talks could address.

- Preaching whose agenda is set by the context cannot transform that context.

- Preaching that is all about me only reinforces my basic problem as a sinner – namely, my tendency to make myself rather than God the centre of all things.

> The culture may ask many questions which are not ultimately of significance at all. But it is only as we take those questions to Scripture that we find God redirecting our thinking and teaching us the real questions we need to ask if we are to engage with eternal realities. This is hard and demanding work. It is also dangerous, because the church is always much more likely to be influenced and infected by the culture in which it is planted than we care to admit. But we are called to minister to real people, to proclaim God's Word in Scripture as it is, his 'now' Word for today's people.[7]

So are we simply to stick to the *text*, then? It all depends on what we think that means. The crucial fact here is one we looked at in Chapter 1 – which is that preaching that is truly biblical will not only have biblical *content*, but it will also have biblical *aims*:

---

[7] David Jackman in Christopher Green & David Jackman [eds.], *When God's Voice is Heard*, (Leicester: IVP, 1995), p. 183.

- We must help the hearers to see why biblical truth *matters*, not just what it *means*. Faithful biblical preaching will always seek to answer the 'so what?' question.

- We cannot be content just to give *information*, because the Bible is intended to bring about our *transformation* (2 Timothy 3:15-17). Faithful biblical preaching will therefore involve exhortation and application as well as explanation.

- Our hearers do not live in *that* world, but in *this* one – so their discipleship cannot be a matter of trying to copy everything Bible characters did. Faithful biblical preaching will not only take the hearers into the Bible, to learn what it teaches us, but will also bring them back into our own situation, to live out what we have learned.

So how can my preaching make contact by being relevant? The short answer is that I must *do exegesis at both ends of the bridge*. I must 'exegete' – that is work out the meaning of – the text, the passage of Scripture on which I will preach. I must also 'exegete' – that is come to understand – the context, the group of people to whom I will preach.

> The preacher must make a good exegesis of his congregation. He must ask how they will receive the text – whether with understanding or incomprehension, belief or questioning, enthusiasm or boredom – and attempt to proceed accordingly. If he fails to do this, he will continually be answering questions nobody present has asked, thereby turning the sermon into a theological conversation – with himself.[8]

We will think more deeply about what this means and how it is done in the next three chapters. For now, we need only note a very simple method of doing exegesis at the people end of the bridge. While I am preparing my talk, I should imagine that there are five or six friends at the table, engaging me in a dialogue about what I am saying and how I am saying it. This group should represent the range of people-types likely to be present in a typical audience: a retired person, a single mother with school-age children, a university student, a tradesperson, someone with a chronic health problem, and so on. Each of them will have a particular perspective from which they will hear and respond to

---

[8]   John Bright, *The Authority of the Old Testament*, (London: SCM, 1967), p. 181.

what I am preparing. I will take each perspective seriously, not to filter out anything the passage says that might be unappealing, but to work out how best to convey the message of that passage. It is not a matter of deciding what to preach but of how best to preach it. I don't want any group represented in the audience to go away feeling that the talk was aimed at someone else.

2.6. *Making contact...by passing the PEST Test*

In order to make effective contact when I preach, my talks must pass the 'PEST Test'! Preaching that enables the hearers to receive, respond to, and remember God's words will need to display four essential characteristics. It will be *Plain, Engaging, Structured,* and *Targeted*. Let us consider what each of these means.

In the first place, preaching that makes contact will be *plain*. Please note that this refers to the *meaning,* not the *style!* Plain preaching is preaching whose meaning is clear and easy to understand, not preaching that is dull. The chief characteristics of *plain* preaching are *simplicity* and *clarity*. What do these look like? And how can I learn to preach like this?

Simplicity will mark a talk only when two prerequisites have been met. The first is that the preacher has a good understanding of the subject matter – I cannot say simply what I do not understand. The second is that the preacher uses language that makes it easy for the hearers to understand the talk. This means that I must employ straightforward, non-technical language. In some places I might be able to get away with such expressions as 'the imminence of the eschatological consummation', but in my preaching I should say that 'the Lord will return soon'!

> All our teaching must be as plain and simple as possible... Truth loves the light, and is most beautiful when most naked.[9]

> There is no substitute in Christian preaching for clear thinking clothed in simple language.[10]

---

[9] Richard Baxter, *The Reformed Pastor*, (Edinburgh: Banner of Truth, 1974 [1656]), p. 115.
[10] John Killinger, *Fundamentals of Preaching*, (Philadelphia: Fortress, 1985), pp. 141, 143.

Christ has spoken in the most simple way and yet he was eloquence personified – therefore the highest eloquence is to speak simply.[11]

An old lady went to hear Bishop JC Ryle preach, and said afterwards that she was very disappointed. She told a friend, 'He's nowt. He's no Bishop. I could understand every word.' Ryle regarded this as the greatest compliment that had ever been paid to his preaching.[12]

It is not enough to be so plain that you can be understood, you must speak so that you cannot be misunderstood.[13]

Clarity is the second characteristic I should be striving for in order to make my preaching plain. How do I achieve it? The answer consists of *four peas!* To be a clear preacher, I need to master Pictures, Pitch, Pruning, and Pace.

Clear preaching is preaching that uses lots of *picture language*. Why is this? Because most of the time most of us think in pictures. It is easy to assume that since we speak in words, we think in words. Yet the boffins tell us this isn't so. It is important to know this, for the most effective communication will be that which conveys the message to the hearers in line with the way we think. In addition, once I have trained myself to speak pictorially, the hearers will think I have used lots of illustrations even if I have not used any.

There is another, even more important reason for using picture language in my preaching, and this is the fact that the Bible itself is highly pictorial in the way it conveys God's Word to us.[14] To give only one example: to speak about God as our protector, the Psalms depict him as a bird who hides us under its wings and feathers (Psalms 17:8; 36:7; 57:1; 91:4). While this must give quite a headache to the literalists, to the rest of us it serves as a vivid portrayal of God's tenderness and personal care for each one of us. Biblical preaching communicates

---

[11]   Martin Luther, quoted in Michael J. Quicke, *360-Degree Preaching*, (Grand Rapids: Baker Academic/Carlisle: Paternoster, 2003), p. 31.

[12]   Told in Eric Russell, *That Man of Granite with the Heart of a Child: Biography of JC Ryle*, (Fearn: Christian Focus, 2001), p. 201.

[13]   Charles H Spurgeon, *Lectures to My Students*, p. 210.

[14]   There is no better presentation of this fact than in Warren Wiersbe, *Preaching and Teaching with Imagination*, (Wheaton: Victor, 1994).

biblical truth in a biblical way, and this means that we should aim to make our preaching as pictorial as the Bible itself. Because the world of the Bible is different from ours in many ways, we will often need to explain the Bible's picture language. But wherever possible we should also use pictures from our world that convey the same meanings as the pictures drawn from the Bible's quite different world. Can you think of an alternative to the image of God as a bird, one that will make the point just as clearly for people unfamiliar with the ways of our feathered friends?

> The best speaker is the one who turns ears into eyes. [Arabic proverb]

> Every time you present a truth, picture it;
> If you would persuade, portray;
> Don't argue, imagine; don't define, depict.
> Remember: no man possesses a truth until he 'sees' it for himself.[15]

Secondly, to be clear my preaching needs to have the right *pitch*. That is, I need to speak at the right level, so that the hearers can grasp what I am saying. Think about another common element of Christian meetings. If the music is pitched too high, the men will find it very difficult to join in the singing, while if it is too low, the women and children will have the same problem. Those in charge of the music have to get the pitch right – and much the same is true of the preacher. I should not aim too high, so that my hearers are left behind, unable to understand what I am saying. But nor should I leave them feeling quite underwhelmed, because I have been simplistic or merely stated the very obvious.

> Christ said, 'Feed my sheep...' Some preachers put the food so high that...[t]hey seem to have read the text, 'Feed my giraffes.'[16]

Thirdly, if they are to be clear, my talks need to be *pruned*. Like clearing a path through the jungle, I must cut away everything that gets in the way. So achieving clarity in my preaching is as much about what I leave out as what I include. I have to learn to be ruthless about pruning everything that distracts the hearers' attention from the main point of

15   R. E. O. White, *A Guide to Preaching*, p. 160.
16   Charles H Spurgeon, quoted in Steve Miller, *C. H. Spurgeon on Spiritual Leadership*, (Chicago: Moody, 2003), p. 149.

the talk, or overloads them, or leads them off at a tangent. I make the truth clear by ensuring that it doesn't have to compete for the hearers' attention with secondary matters.

> Anything that doesn't help hurts. Everything in the sermon should contribute to furthering the purpose. If it doesn't make it clearer, more memorable, more persuasive, it hinders.[17]

> ...clarity and simplicity are essential for effective sermons, and they will never emerge without bold editing. Good preaching is characterized by what is not said almost as much as by what is said. Powerful sermons arise from courageous editing.[18]

Finally, to be clear I need to preach at the right *pace*. If I pump out the content faster than the hearers can handle, I will soon leave them behind and they will not get the message. One essential key to the right pace, therefore, is good use of the *pause*.

> Pauses or moments of silence provide powerful breaks in sermon delivery that allow the audience time to mull over what you just said. Pauses also can communicate emphasis and focus.[19]

> Pauses are the major punctuation marks of speech. Pauses are 'thoughtful silences.' They go beyond a mere stoppage in speech and give the audience a brief opportunity to think, feel, and respond.[20]

A second key is effective use of *repetition*. This applies primarily to the main points of the talk – as they are repeated at intervals throughout the talk, my hearers can catch up or get back on board if they have wandered off.

> Try to build into your talks places where you pause and *briefly* recap what you have said...The best places to do this are at the end of major sections...This practice is valuable for communication because it both reminds the audience of the structure of the message (and thus aids comprehension of the

---

[17]   Jay E. Adams, *Truth Apparent*, (Phillipsburg, NJ: P & R, 1982), p. 19.
[18]   Michael J. Quicke, *360-Degree Preaching*, p. 178.
[19]   Terry G. Carter, J. Scott Duvall, J. Daniel Hays, *Preaching God's Word*, (Grand Rapids: Zondervan, 2005), p. 156.
[20]   Haddon W. Robinson, *Biblical Preaching*, 2nd ed. (Grand Rapids: Baker Academic, 2001), p. 217.

material) and repeats the key points (thus helping the audience remember them).[21]

What of the second point of the 'PEST Test'? Preaching that makes contact is *engaging*. What does this involve? First and foremost, it is not engaging if it is boring! So how can I ensure that my preaching is not boring? I must *say gripping things in a gripping way*. But what does this mean? 'Saying gripping things' means speaking about things that obviously matter – which will be the case if I am expounding the Bible. My hearers need to sense, first, that these are things that matter greatly to me, and secondly, that these things should matter to them just as much. Saying these things 'in a gripping way' means using language that is clear, vivid, and direct. It also means speaking directly to my hearers – not just talking in their general direction, but seeking to grip them, to convince them, and to move them to respond rightly.

> As we open texts of Scripture we have a case to present, an appeal to make, a truth to press on the heart, and a response to solicit. Our preaching will be far more vigorous when we work hard to convince, persuade, reason, motivate and convict people of the truth with which we are dealing.[22]

> The words you use can be *predictable* on the one hand or have *impact* on the other...High predictability will result in low impact...Work for freshness...High impact requires low predictability.[23]

Preaching also fails to be engaging when it allows the hearers to remain passive. Although a Bible talk is usually a monologue, it communicates most effectively when it doesn't feel like one. Good preaching feels like a dialogue, because it gives the hearers a sense of *participation*. It involves them.

How can I learn to engage my hearers when I preach? One obvious way of doing so is to use 'we' and 'us' instead of only saying 'you'. Even when they do not register this consciously, this gives the hearers a sense of being involved with me in something that concerns all of us. But if I only use 'you' it will feel to them as though they are being spoken at,

---

[21] James Rye, *The Communicator's Craft*, (Leicester: IVP, 1990), p. 108f.
[22] Murray A. Capill, *Preaching with Spiritual Vigour*, p. 142.
[23] Wayne V. McDill, *The Moment of Truth*, p. 160f.

not spoken to. (Worse still, it might give the impression that I do not think that what the Bible passage teaches applies to me!)

> ...we are both hearer and speaker of every sermon we preach. The word is not just from us; it is also for us.[24]

Secondly, I can involve my hearers by asking questions and not just making declarations. Instead of saying, 'In verse 4 Paul tells us that...', I could say, 'Can you see what Paul is doing in verse 4? Look how he...' The difference between these two approaches might seem too slight to be significant – but if the second one is a regular feature of the way I communicate with my hearers, they will have a much greater sense of involvement in my talks.

Thirdly, I will engage my hearers by anticipating their reactions and putting them into words. When they hear me voice what they are thinking, my hearers will have a much greater sense of involvement in what I am saying. They will listen more keenly, not only because they will now feel that the preacher understands them, but because they will want to know how I respond to their questions and struggles.

> ...it is part of the teacher's task not just to reveal what is hidden and to solve knotty problems but also, while doing this, to anticipate other questions which may arise, in case they undermine or refute what we are saying...[25]

Fourthly, I give my hearers a sense of involvement by stating the implications in a direct and personal way rather than leaving them vague and general. It should be, 'This faces us with a very clear choice, doesn't it? And one that we need to face today.' 'There are some important implications here' is nowhere near sharp or clear enough. If the way I state the applications makes them sound as though they are meant for everybody in general, everyone present is likely to assume that they are meant for someone else!

One final comment about preaching that fails to be engaging. My hearers will cease being involved if my talks are either too overloaded or too long. Either way, if the quantity is simply too great for them to handle they will eventually tune out. This is where I need to

---

[24] Charles B. Bugg, *Preaching From the Inside Out*, (Nashville: Broadman, 1992), p. 23.

[25] Augustine, *On Christian Teaching*, (Oxford World's Classics), (Oxford: OUP, 1997 [ca.425 AD]), p. 127.

'exegete' my audience – wherever possible, I need to know them well enough to know what their capacity is.

The third part of the 'PEST Test' is this: preaching that makes contact is *structured*. It has a framework that is clearly evident to the hearers, an outline they can easily discern and follow.

> Listeners more readily grasp ideas that have been formed and pulled together. It is easier to catch a baseball than a handful of sand...[26]

Why is this important? For the simple reason that preaching is *heard,* not *read*. The difference between these two methods of receiving communication is of fundamental importance, and it is vital that we preachers understand it. Think about the difference between hearing a lecture on a certain subject and reading a magazine article on the same subject. The principal difference, the one that leads to all the others, is that in the speaking situation *the speaker is sovereign,* while in the reading situation *the reader rules*. When I listen to speakers, I must go at *their* pace; when I am reading, I can go at *my* pace. If the speaker makes a point I don't understand, I can't afford to stop listening while I work out what she meant. But when a writer makes a point I don't understand, I can re-read the piece until I do, or put it aside and return to it hours or even days later.

As a preacher, it is vital that I understand the importance of enabling my hearers to keep up, and also of providing 'markers' that give them a sense of where we are.

> Congregations need an outline...A sermon which has an orderly, consistent progress aids the listener's memory...Good outlines state the point in clear, crisp style...[like] John Wesley's sermon on stewardship with its three points, 'Earn all you can, Save all you can, Give all you can'...[27]

This should mean that the hearers feel as though they are accompanying me on a step-by-step journey through the passage.

> The special nature of oral communication...requires you to plan

---

[26] Bryan Chapell, *Christ-Centered Preaching,* 2nd ed., (Grand Rapids: Baker Academic, 2005), p. 45.

[27] J. Daniel Baumann, *An Introduction to Contemporary Preaching,* (Grand Rapids: Baker, 1972), p. 150.

your sermon carefully as an unfolding sequence of ideas in time. Like a walk in the countryside, your sermon must take your hearer step-by-step along the journey of thought in a way that gets his attention and keeps his interest.[28]

We can think of the points in my outline as the stepping-stones that enable us to cross a creek or the rungs that enable us to climb a ladder. Secondly, having a structure that is evident to the hearers enables them to 'get back on board' if they lose concentration for a short while, or if they don't understand a particular point. In short, the structure of my talk provides both *steps* and *prompts* for my hearers.

> We must learn to be teachers. Not lecturers, but clear, incisive, logical, compelling teachers. If people cannot follow the drift of a message, cannot see how the flow of the message has unfolded, and cannot have some retention of the main points, we have failed.[29]

How should I structure my talks? There are three simple guidelines to follow. First, the structure should be *appropriate*. That is, the passage itself should determine the contents and shape of my outline. I must derive the outline from the passage, not impose it on the passage. Secondly, the structure should be *modest*, as opposed to lavish. It needs to be 'hearer-friendly', by not being too complex or detailed. The more I put into my talk outlines the easier it is for my hearers to get lost. Thirdly, the structure of my talks should be *varied:* they mustn't become predictable – because then people will not be so eager to listen. Not only that, but if the outlines of all of my talks have three points ending in 'ation', then my hearers would be quite justified in concluding that I wasn't getting the outlines from the passage.

There is another reason for putting time and effort into structuring our talks. This is so that our hearers can remember them, and so go on benefiting from the talks after they have heard them. Our slogan here is, *If it is worth saying, it is worth remembering!*

We will look at this matter more thoroughly in Chapters 4 and 5. But to help us to start thinking it through, you might like to assess the suitability of the following talk outlines. (To protect the guilty, I will not

---

[28] Wayne V. McDill, *The Moment of Truth*, p. 158.
[29] Murray A. Capill, *Preaching with Spiritual Vigour*, p. 137.

say where I found them – but none of them comes from me!)

Psalm 23

1. A relationship that is precious ('my shepherd')
2. A resource that is plentiful ('I shall not want')
3. A rest that is pleasant ('pastures...waters')
4. A restoration that is perfect ('he restores my soul')
5. A righteousness that is practical ('...paths of righteousness')
6. A reassurance that is personal ('You are with me')
7. A repast that is peaceful ('a table before me')
8. A recovery that is powerful ('oil...cup')
9. A realization that is phenomenal ('follow me')
10. A regularity that is positive ('all the days')
11. A reward that is perennial ('the house of the Lord forever')

2 Timothy 4:1-8

1. Paul's Charge (vv. 1-2)

   - Definition of a charge (v. 1)
   - Description of the charge (v. 2)

2. Paul's Caution (vv. 3-4)

   - Caution against false doctrine (v. 3)
   - Caution against false teachers (v. 3)
   - Caution against false religions (v. 3)

3. Paul's Concern (v. 5)

   - That Timothy endure afflictions (v. 5)
   - That Timothy evangelize (v. 5)
   - That Timothy prove his ministry (v. 5)

4. Paul's Confidence (v. 7)

   - That he fought a good fight (v. 7)
   - That he finished his course (v. 7)
   - That he kept the faith (v. 7)

5. Paul's Crown (v. 8)

   - The purpose of the crown: righteousness (v. 8)
   - The person of the crown: the Righteous Judge (v. 8)

The Good Samaritan (Luke 10:25-37)

Three philosophies of life:

    1.   The robbers: 'What's yours is mine – I'll take it.'
    2.   The priest and the Levite: 'What's ours is ours – we'll keep it.'
    3.   The Samaritan: 'What's mine is ours – I'll share it.'

The Prodigal Son (Luke 15:11-24)

1. Sick of home   2. Homesick   3. Home

1. I want!   2. I am in want   3. I am wanted

    A.   *His madness*

- He wanted his tin
- He surrendered to sin
- He abandoned his kin

    B.   *His badness*

- He went to the dogs
- He ate with the hogs
- He pawned all his togs

    C.   *His gladness*

- He was given the seal
- He ate up the veal
- He danced the reel

The final part of the 'PEST Test', the fourth characteristic of preaching that makes contact, is that it is *targeted*. It aims to have an *impact*, because the Bible does.[30] This has a direct bearing on the way we word the main points in the talk outline. The lecturer uses an abstract, impersonal format, but the preacher should use a concrete, personal style.

Contrast the two (oversimplified) outlines:

---

[30]   See, for example, Romans 15:4; 1 Corinthians 10:11-12; 1 Thessalonians 2:9-13; 4:1-3; 2 Timothy 3:16-17.

Lecture outline:

    1.   The Duty of Intercessory Prayer
    2.   The Purpose of Intercessory Prayer
    3.   The Results of Intercessory Prayer

Preaching outline:

    1.   God commands *you* to pray for others.
    2.   God commands you to pray for *others*.
    3.   God commands you to pray for others' *needs*.

> The outlines above cover roughly the same material. But the first is analytical; it discusses the 'nature' of intercessory prayer. The second is motivational; it discusses God's command to the congregation to pray for others. Do you see the difference?[31]

The fact that our preaching should be targeted is not just a matter of how we word our outlines; it concerns the nature of preaching itself. Preaching is not simply a matter of declaration, a take-it-or-leave-it announcement; it aims to persuade the hearers, so that they both receive and respond to what has been declared. As exposition of the Bible, our preaching must be in line with the passage's purpose as well as its teaching – not only what it says, but why it says what it says.

> The purpose of preaching is not simply to discuss a subject, but to achieve an object. A true sermon involves not only explanation but also application.[32]
>
> [The preacher should] address himself to the heart, so as to flash the light of the Gospel into the spirit of the hearer, and to bend his will...to the truth.[33]

This brings us to the end of our all-too-brief discussion of preaching principles. Now we are going to turn our attention to the process of preparing and preaching a Bible talk. I call the stages in this process (1) discovering (2) digesting (3) designing (4) defining and – as the completion of the process – (5) delivering the talk. I could have called

---

[31]   Jay E. Adams, *Truth Apparent*, p. 51.

[32]   Warren & David Wiersbe, *The Elements of Preaching*, (Wheaton: Tyndale House, 1986), p. 23.

[33]   John Wyclif, quoted in Benson Bobrick, *Wide as the Waters: The Story of the English Bible and the Revolution It Inspired*, (New York: Simon & Schuster, 2001), p. 50.

the first three Assembling, Absorbing, and Arranging; or Exploration, Percolation, and Compilation; or maybe... (And now you know something important about what I do with the main points in my talks!)

As we work our way through these stages in the following chapters, we will be constructing a talk based on Matthew 6:5-13. I have chosen this as our sample passage because it contains material that is very familiar. This means that we can concentrate on working out how to preach it, instead of getting bogged down trying to work out what it means.

Are you ready? Then let's go to work!

GOT IT?

i.   What are the two areas in which expository preachers should work hard?

ii.   What is the problem with describing preaching as 'Bible-teaching'?

iii. Will good preaching be relevant?

iv.   What is the 'PEST Test'?

v.   What are the four peas that determine the clarity of our preaching?

vi.   Why do my talks need to have a clear structure?

PART 2

PROCESS

Introductory thoughts

This section of the book is devoted to *one essential point* – that preparing a Bible talk is a *process*, not an event. Treating it as something that I can do in one session will inevitably lead to poor preaching. In fact, preparation is best seen as requiring *four stages* that are spread over at least *two sessions* – three sessions if at all possible. While it is unlikely that we will always manage to get three sessions for preparing a Bible talk, we *must* try as hard as we possibly can to get two sessions. Why is this? Because it is (nearly always) impossible to do the whole job in just one session. Then what is 'the whole job'? What are the four stages in the preparation process? They are *discovering* and *digesting* (Chapter 3); *designing* (Chapter 4); and *defining* (Chapter 5). Chapter 6 (*delivering*) covers the final stage of the entire process – the actual preaching of the talk that I have prepared.

How much time do I have to put into this process? How long should it take to prepare a Bible talk? The first answer we must give is this: 'It all depends!' Talks are unpredictable. Some come quickly, and some seem reluctant to appear at all. It is important, therefore, that you don't look upon the contents of the next three chapters as *a formula that will guarantee success*. If you like, think of it instead as a *recipe* that in my experience usually works quite well. The implied cooking analogy is actually quite useful, for three reasons.

i.   Just as cooking involves flair and not just formulae, preaching is not a matter of slavishly following rules.

ii.   Yet, as every beginning chef knows, there's a great deal to be said for sticking closely to the recipe the first few times you make the dish. Flair is fine – when you have enough experience to know what works and what doesn't. As a novice preacher, I will find that it pays to use the recipe, until I don't need to use it any more.

iii. As every collector of recipes knows, everybody's Grandma has a different way of making the Christmas cake! The recipe we will work our way through in these chapters is not the only way of learning how to preach – but it will help you to produce appetizing, nourishing meals that feed God's family.

My second answer assumes that the question is asking how long it takes the *typical* preacher to prepare a *normal* Bible talk to be preached in the *usual* setting! I think we ought to give it as much time as possible – but on average I should expect to take around three hours for each of stages 1, 3 and 4. This means that it will usually take about ten hours to prepare a Bible talk. As I get more experience, this average will probably come down a bit.

One way of saving some time in preparation, and something that every preacher should have, is a preaching file or book. This is where I write down everything – ideas for talk outlines or illustrations, quotable quotes, anecdotes – that I might be able to use in my preaching.

> To enable sermons to grow we must cultivate a seed-book, where *every* idea for a sermon gets *written down*, fixed, captured, and recorded, without fail ...[1]

This is only a time-saver if I can find material quickly and easily. If I create a system that requires lots of time for recording and then retrieving material, I have defeated the purpose.

What I have just said alerts you to something I need to explain. I had been preaching for more than twenty years before I got my first computer. As a result, I still do my preparation in ways that might seem very odd to those of you who don't predate the computer. So when I refer to such things as pens, paper, writing, and books, you will need to translate it into the right equivalent in computer-speak!

---

[1]   R. E. O. White, *A Guide to Preaching*, p. 66.

3. Discovering and Digesting

3.1. Discovering and Digesting: To get you thinking...

Some people say it's impossible these days to hold people's attention for a half-hour monologue. But they forget that the most popular stand-up comedians manage it – despite being profane and worldly – with material they've worked on for two months. So why shouldn't most preachers manage it with a few hours' prep on Saturday afternoon and the miraculous empowerment of Almighty God? After all, which is more truly interesting, the eternal mysteries of salvation, or some pointless rubbish about whether you've ever noticed that when you're in a queue at the supermarket the other always goes quicker? I rest my case. (The answer is 'the eternal mysteries of salvation'.)

Rev'd Gerald Ambulance, *My Ministry Manual,* p. 34.

He knows how diligent Timothy is, and yet he recommends to him a persevering reading of the Scriptures. For how can pastors teach others unless they themselves are able to learn...? Woe to the slothfulness of those who do not peruse the oracles of the Spirit day and night to learn from them how to discharge their office...In addition, in case leisurely reading should be thought enough, he shows that what he reads he must also use and tells him to attend to teaching and exhortation...We should notice the order, how he mentions reading before teaching and exhortation, for Scripture is the source of all wisdom and pastors ought to draw from it all that they set before their flock.

John Calvin, *Calvin's NT Commentaries,* 10.246-7 (on 1 Timothy 4:13).

'It must be so interesting to preach to the Brethren, Cousin Amos. I quite envy you. Do you prepare your sermon beforehand or do you just make it up as you go along?'...'Doan't 'ee speak o' the word o' the Lord in that godless way, as though 'twere one o' they pagan tales...The word is not prepared beforehand; it falls on me mind like the manna fell from heaven into the bellies of the starving Israelites.' 'Really! How interesting. Then you have no idea what you are going to say before you get there?' 'Ay...I allus knows 'twill be summat about burnin'...or the eternal torment...or sinners comin' to judgement. But I don't know exactly what the words will be until I gets up in me seat and looks round at all their sinful faces, awaitin' all eager for to hear me. Then I knows what I mun say, and I says it.'

Stella Gibbons, Cold Comfort Farm, (Camberwell: Penguin, 2009 [1932]), p. 89.

Some pastors and preachers are lazy and no good. They do not pray; they do not study; they do not read; they do not study the Scripture... The call is: watch, study, attend to reading... [Y]ou cannot read too much in Scripture, what you read you cannot read too carefully, what you read carefully you cannot understand too well, what you understand well, you cannot teach too well, what you teach well you cannot live too well... Therefore dear ... pastors and preachers, pray, read, study, be diligent... This evil, shameful time is no season for being lazy, for sleeping, and snoring.

Martin Luther, quoted in FW Meuser, 'Luther as Preacher of the Word of God' in Donald K. McKim [ed.], The Cambridge Companion to Martin Luther, (CUP, 2003), p. 144f.

Expository preaching is a most exacting discipline. Perhaps that is why it is so rare... It will not be enough to skim through a few verses in daily Bible reading, nor to study a passage only when we have to preach from it... We must daily soak ourselves in the Scriptures... We shall need strength of mind to eschew short cuts. We must spend time studying our text with painstaking thoroughness, meditating on it, wrestling with it, worrying at it as a dog with a bone, until it yields its meaning; and sometimes this process will be accompanied by toil and tears.

John Stott, The Preacher's Portrait, p. 27.

3.2. Discovering and Digesting: Guidance from Scripture

Oh how I love your law! I meditate on it all day long... How sweet are your words to my taste, sweeter than honey to my mouth!...Your word is a lamp to my feet and a light for my path...give me understanding according to your word.

Psalm 119:97, 103, 105, 169.

Did you hear about the mosquito that strayed into a nudist colony? It ended up having a nervous breakdown because although it knew what it was supposed to do, it couldn't decide where to begin! If I am not to suffer the same fate, I must know how to begin my preparation. So how do I get from Point A to Point B? How do I start with a Bible passage and end up with a talk I preach to my hearers?

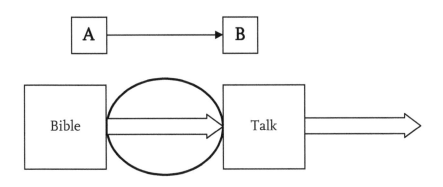

Before we get immersed in the details of this process, there is something that is simply too important to leave unsaid. It is this: I must put my preparation into *the right context*. And what is that? An ever-deepening personal devotion to God my Saviour, in which I feed on his Word and call upon him in prayer daily, seeking to grow steadily in my love for him, my likeness to him, and my loyalty to him.

If I have a regular preaching ministry, then there are other essential ingredients that should also form part of my context. I need to grow in loving and serving those to whom I preach – which must involve listening to them and learning from them, so that I begin to see the world through their eyes. I also need to have a discipline of personal study, so that I continue to grow in my understanding of God's Word and its implications for the issues of life. And so on...

What needs to be emphasized here is an absolutely fundamental principle: I must be going to the Bible *daily as a believer*, and not just *weekly as a preacher*. My use of the Bible in preparing talks must be in this larger context, in which I am reading, understanding, appropriating, and obeying God's Word every day.

If you continue to learn, your people will be the beneficiaries. If you stop, they will suffer the consequences.[1]

...the preacher is a 'distributor' rather than a 'manufacturer'. For this reason, we must be devoted to the Word of God, meditating on it daily, studying it systematically, reading it continually, and always feeding our own souls and preparing to feed our people.[2]

...good preaching begins, continues, and ends on our knees... Preaching is a spiritual exercise that requires a spiritual dependence of the preacher...on the Spirit and Word of God.[3]

3.3. Discovering

This *first stage* in the process of preparation is where I dig into a Bible passage, in order to discover what it is teaching.

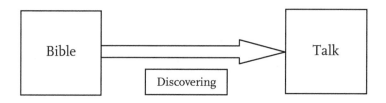

This means that the first step on the way to *exposition* is *exegesis*. In order to preach a Bible talk that faithfully conveys what God says to us in this passage, we must work hard at understanding it thoroughly. Before we look at *how* I do this, we need to think about *where* I do it.

---

[1]   Reid Ferguson, *The Little Book of Things You Should Know about Ministry*, (Fearn: Christian Focus, 2002), p. 52.

[2]   Warren W. Wiersbe, *The Dynamics of Preaching*, p. 24f.

[3]   Keith Willhite, *Preaching with Relevance without Dumbing Down*, (Grand Rapids: Kregel, 2001), pp. 132-3.

3.3.1. Discovering...where?

Surely the answer is obvious! I do my preparation at my desk. This might make it harder than it needs to be, however. Most of us have cluttered desks, and some of the clutter is work we are under pressure to finish. Such a workspace will make it very difficult for me to give the Bible passage my undivided attention. What I need is a clear desk or table, where I can spread out my open Bible(s) and my writing paper, and (later on) my commentaries and other reference books. Where there is nothing except what I use in preparing it, there is nothing to distract me from my talk. This workspace also needs to be fairly quiet – somewhere I am not going to be disturbed.

> Study your text at a clean desk. Allow no competing sources of stimulation. Have before you only the open Bible and minimal tools. The clean desk – devoid of notes, reminders, and memos – aids concentration.[4]

3.3.2. Discovering...how?

Once I have prepared a suitable workspace, I set to work on the passage, writing down every idea that comes to me. Although much of what I write at this initial stage will probably be discarded later, for now I am like a squirrel collecting and hoarding nuts for the long winter ahead.

> Study with a clean sheet of paper before you...Study with a pen in hand. Record most of the ideas and pictures that rush to your head – and those that come slowly too. Who knows what will actually become useful?...Be prepared to spend two hours examining the passage without commentaries.[5]

But where do I find the nuts? How do I generate the ideas I am meant to record for possible use later? *The* key (humanly speaking) to cracking open the meaning of any passage is hitting it with the right questions.

> I keep six honest serving-men; (They taught me all I knew)
> Their names are What and Where and When and How and Why

---

[4] Donald E. Demaray, *Proclaiming the Truth*, (Grand Rapids: Baker, 1979), p. 27.
[5] Donald E. Demaray, *Proclaiming the Truth*, p. 27.

and Who.[6]

One way of stating these questions for our purposes is as follows:

i.   What does the passage say? What is its point?

ii.   How does it say this? What is its style and approach?

iii. Why does it say this? What is its purpose?

iv.   Where (in its book) and when (in history) does it say this?

v.   By saying this, thus (in this way, and for this reason), there (in this literary context), and then (in this historical period), what did it mean to the original recipients?

vi.   What message is there for us now in what was said to them then?

We are going to use a simpler way of asking the questions:

i.   What is the passage talking about? That is, what is the point of the passage? This is where I identify the 'big idea' of the passage, its subject. This will give me the focus of my talk.

ii.   *What is the passage saying about what it is talking about?* That is, what are the points in the passage?

      This is where I identify the specific things the passage is saying. This means investigating the structure as well as the content of the passage. This will give me the *framework* of my talk.

iii. *What is the passage doing with what it is saying?* That is, where does the passage point?

      This is where I identify the function of the passage – is it informing or reminding, encouraging or warning, praising or correcting, inspiring or ...? This will give me the *flavour* of my talk, the way I apply it.

By means of these questions, my aim is to analyse the passage and discover its message. This has to be where I begin, for what the passage is saying has to be in charge throughout the entire process of preparing the talk and delivering it to my hearers. Only then will my preaching be

---

[6]   Rudyard Kipling, *Just So Stories*, (London: Minster Classics, 1968), p. 47.

faithfully biblical.

> You must discover the meaning of the words and of the whole statement...In order to arrive at this you will have to learn to ask questions of your text...Ask such questions as, Why did he say that? Why did he say it in this particular way? What is he getting at? What was his object and purpose? One of the first things a preacher has to learn is to talk to his texts...But at the same time never force your text. An idea may occur to you and it may excite you and thrill you; but if you find that you have to do some manipulating or forcing in order to make that fit into this particular text, don't do it. You must sacrifice a good sermon rather than force a text.[7]

This section sets out a simple procedure for doing this *exegesis:* that is, for analysing and interpreting a passage of Scripture. It is important to note that this procedure covers only the basic steps that need to be taken – in other words, what follows does not give a comprehensive account of all that exegesis involves. The *discovery* process I am recommending has three stages: *reading, referring,* and *reviewing.*

Discovering...by Reading (and Writing)

The first of these can be done in three simple steps. The *first step* is to write the passage out line by line. Make a separate line for each additional point the passage is making. Trying to work out what to put on each line means that you have already begun working out what the passage means by what it says.

> *When you pray do not be like the hypocrites*
>
> *for they love to pray standing in the synagogues*
>
> *and on the street corners*
>
> *to be seen by others.*
>
> *Truly I tell you, they have received their reward in full.*
>
> *But when you pray, go into your room, close the door*

---

[7]   Martyn Lloyd-Jones, *Preaching and Preachers,* pp. 201-2.

and pray to your Father

who is unseen.

Then your Father

who sees what is done in secret

will reward you.

And when you pray, do not keep on babbling like pagans

for they think they will be heard

because of their many words.

Do not be like them

for your Father knows what you need

before you ask him.

So this is how you should pray:

our Father in heaven

your name be honoured

your kingdom come

your will be done

on earth as it is in heaven.

Give us this day our daily bread

and forgive us our debts

as we also have forgiven our debtors

and lead us not into temptation

but deliver us from the evil one.

The *second step* is to indent the lines so that I distinguish the main statements from the secondary statements. These will depend on the main statements in some way – explaining them, or giving an example, or indicating an exception, and so on. The main statements should be against the left-hand margin of the page, and the other statements are indented to line up with the particular words to which they are most connected.

When you pray do not be like the hypocrites

         for they love to pray standing in the synagogues

                and on the street corners

                        to be seen by others.

      Truly I tell you, they have received their reward in full.

But when you pray, go into your room, close the door

      and pray to your Father

            who is unseen.

        Then your Father

           who sees what is done in secret

                 will reward you.

And when you pray, do not keep on babbling like pagans

      for they think they will be heard

              because of their many words.

    Do not be like them

      for your Father knows what you need

              before you ask him.

So this is how you should pray:

Our Father in heaven

    Your name be honoured

    Your kingdom come

    Your will be done

        on earth as it is in heaven

    Give us this day our daily bread

    and forgive us our debts

        as we also have forgiven our debtors

    Lead us not into temptation

        But deliver us from evil.

The *third step* is to mark the page in a way that draws attention to all of the significant features of the passage. You can do this by using underlining, or colours, or enclosing words in boxes, or whatever. The aim is to show which elements in the passage are linked with each other.

When you pray do not be like the hypocrites

>> for they love to pray standing in the synagogues

>>> and on the street corners

>> to be <u>seen</u> by others.

>> Truly I tell you, they have received their reward in full.

But when you pray, go into your room, close the door

> and pray to your Father

>> who is <u>unseen</u>.

> Then your Father

>> who <u>sees</u> what is done in secret

>>> will reward you.

And when you pray, do not keep on <u>babbling</u> like pagans

>> for they think they will be <u>heard</u>

>>> because of their many <u>words</u>.

> Do not be like them

>> for your Father knows what you need

>>> before you <u>ask</u> him.

So this is how you should pray...

By the time I have done this carefully, all kinds of ideas and questions will have occurred to me. I might have discovered that I need to research the meaning of something referred to in the passage. I might have had some ideas about a focus for my talk, or even a possible outline or two. It is important that I write down *everything* I think of during this stage of the process. I can't afford to discard anything at all yet!

As I consider what the marked page above tells me, I might write down something like this:

- The passage tells us twice not to be like a certain kind of pray-er.

- The problem with the first group has to do with *sight* – being seen.

- The problem with the second group has to do with *sound* – being heard.

- The reason we must not pray like these two groups is that we are praying to our Father.

- We should not want our praying to be seen by others, because we are not performing but praying to our Father – and he sees.

- We should not think that God will not take action to help us until we impress him with our praying, because he is our Father – and he knows.

- Right praying calls upon God as our Father in heaven.

- Right praying gives priority to God's name and kingdom and will.

- Right praying asks for our needs to be met.

Before I move on to the next stage, it is a good idea to read through the passage in one or two mainstream Bible translations different from the one I normally use. This will sometimes alert me to other features of the passage I need to consider.

Once I have done this, I might finish this part of my *discovering* work by writing out a list of things I need to investigate, to make sure I know what they mean. My list might look like this:

- Why do pagans think that the quantity of words they produce will determine whether their prayers are heard?

- What does it mean for God to be 'in heaven'?

- What does God's 'name' refer to – and how is it 'hallowed'?

- Why do we ask only for our 'daily' bread?

- What are our 'debts' to God, for which we need to be forgiven?

- If we didn't ask him not to, would God 'lead us into temptation'?

Discovering...by Referring

When I have finished writing out all that seems important, I am now ready to move into the next major section of my *discovering* work – namely, *getting out my toolkit*. The tools are the kind of reference books that will help me understand the passage better. So the tools I will want to use now are some good commentaries on the passage and perhaps also a Bible dictionary. There are two things about this I need to explain. First, what makes a 'good' commentary? The answer is, one that helps me to understand the passage better than I did. This will be because it explains the meaning of what is in the passage – by showing how the passage fits into its immediate context; by explaining its words and phrases, and any people or customs it refers to; by analysing any quotations it contains (from the Old Testament or elsewhere); and so on. It will not focus on how we apply the passage's teaching – although a good commentary will give some indications of how we can do this. Rather, it will focus on explaining, first, what the passage means by what it says, and second, what the passage is doing with what it says.

The second thing I need to explain is why it is important not to get out my commentaries any sooner than this. One of the easiest traps to fall into, not least because it seems like a good way of saving time, is to read the passage once or twice, and then to read my commentaries. The first problem here is that I won't get much benefit out of the commentaries if I do this. That is not because there is anything wrong with them, but because I haven't done enough work on the passage to realize why I need to know what they are telling me. They will be answering questions about the passage that I don't yet have, or explaining features of it that I haven't yet noticed. It is only when I do my own discovery work on the passage first that I create enough windows through which the commentaries can shine their light. There is another problem with going to the commentaries too soon. When I do so, I fail to immerse myself in the passage and get inside it so that it can get inside me.

Using commentaries at the outset can diminish personal immersion in the text and lead preachers to treat Scripture as something to be read about or thought about through *other* people's thoughts rather than something to be encountered directly as God-breathed words...[8]

Discovering...by Reviewing

When I have finished going through the commentaries, I now need to take stock of my progress in understanding the passage. Am I ready to move out of the exegesis phase and to begin preparing the talk itself? A very helpful way of assessing where I am is to write myself a brief 'progress report', summarizing what I think the passage means and itemising those features of it that I do not yet understand sufficiently. If the items on the list are too important or too numerous to ignore, then I need to turn to additional resources – other commentaries, Bible dictionaries and so on – to give me a good grasp of what the passage means.

The best way of doing this is to use the three questions we identified earlier. This is where I write down my answers to these questions. My page might look something like this:

i.   What is the passage about? What is its 'big idea'?

Prayer.

ii.   What is it saying about what it is about?

Jesus is teaching his disciples not to pray wrongly, but to pray to their Father in heaven. He mentions two wrong approaches to prayer, one aimed at impressing those who see, the other at winning a hearing. He then teaches the right approach, giving a prayer outline that first prays for God and then prays for ourselves.

iii.   What is it doing with what it is saying?

It is warning against the wrong praying of the hypocrites and the pagans, and it is showing how to pray the right way.

My aim is to reach the point where I am sure I have grasped the 'big idea' of the passage, and I can clearly express the focus and aim of the talk. So at this stage in my work on the passage, I might try to express what I have learned about the passage so far in a one-sentence

---

[8]   Michael J. Quicke, *360-Degree Preaching*, p. 142.

summary. This might be, 'This passage urges disciples not to pray the wrong way but to pray the right way, with their praying controlled by the fact that it is directed to our Father in heaven.' One way of making sure that I have got this as clear and sharp as I can is to imagine that I have to write the headline for a newspaper report of my talk. (Would *'Jesus puts prayer to the Father-in-heaven test'* do the job?)

Once I have completed the *discovering* stage of the process adequately, then I can move on to the *digesting* stage. Before we consider what this involves, let us just remind ourselves of what *the three Rs of discovering* involve:

i.   I read the passage and write it out

- to find out what it says
- to find out what I don't understand

ii. I refer to the tools in my tool-kit

- this needs to be the second task, not the first
- they need to be the right tools for getting the job done

iii. I review what I have done

- what is now clear to me?
- what isn't clear yet? Are these important enough for me to repeat step ii.?

3.4.   *Digesting*

This *second stage* in the process of preparing a Bible talk is where I give myself time to *absorb* what I have learned.

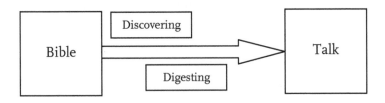

One of the most crucial parts of the preparation process is the one in which I am not (consciously) preparing! Once I have put significant time and effort into the passage, it will keep bubbling away in my mind while I go about my daily tasks. It is during this time that the passage is on the back burner that some of my most important ideas and insights will come. Conversely, if I move straight from exegesis of the passage into preparation of the talk, I will be trying to decide how to explain and apply to others truths I have not had time to digest.

This is such an important part of the process that I recommend leaving at least one day, and preferably two, before attempting to turn the fruits of my exegesis into a talk.

The *digesting* stage creates space for two important processes, *chewing* and *choosing,* to occur.

3.4.1.   Chewing over the teaching of the passage and taking it in.

This is where I imitate a cow or a goat! I let my mind do with the Bible passage what these animals do with what they have eaten. I need to turn it over and over in my mind, looking at it from various angles, until I have seen all that there is to see (on this occasion!) and until the truths being taught there have taken hold of me. While this is happening, I should be preaching the passage to myself, considering how to apply to myself and appropriate for myself what it teaches. This is what the Puritans meant by 'meditation', and it is an absolutely essential part of any preacher's process of preparation.

> Puritan meditation on Scripture was modelled on the Puritan sermon; in meditation the Puritan would seek to search and challenge his heart, stir his affections to hate sin and love righteousness, and encourage himself with God's promises, just as Puritan preachers would do from the pulpit.[9]

> A sermon...can never be well preached, until it has been first preached to ourselves...To bear our message written upon our hearts, is the best method of conveying to our people deep and weighty impressions of the things of God.[10]

One of the principal aims of this digesting process, and one of the sure signs that it is occurring, is that the substance of the passage arouses in

---

9   J. I. Packer, *A Quest for Godliness: The Puritan Vision of the Christian Life,* (Wheaton: Crossway, 1990), p. 24.

10   Charles Bridges, *The Christian Ministry,* (London: Banner of Truth, 1967 [1830]), p. 157f.

me the very responses that I long to see in those who hear my talk. I cannot expect my talks to affect my hearers in ways that they have not affected me first.

> Wood that is capable of burning is not set alight unless fire is put to it. Similarly anyone who would encourage godly affections and desires in others must first have godly affections within himself. Thus, whatever responses a particular sermon requires should first be stirred up privately in our own minds, so that we can kindle the same flame in our hearers.[11]

3.4.2.   Choosing the best pathway through the passage for my talk.

My first thoughts about how to preach the passage may leave a lot to be desired! It is vital that I give myself enough time to discover their defects and to discern other, better ways of tackling it. One of the key issues I face is deciding *how much* of what I have learned about the passage should go into the talk. I need to be sure that I preach only *one* Bible talk, not two or three pretending to be one! This means that I need to be clear about the *big idea*. That is, I need to know what the passage is about – what is its centre, its focus, its subject?

Another key issue the *digesting* stage can help me with is deciding how *I* can best preach the message of the passage. There might be ways of tackling it that would be very helpful, if I could preach that way. If I am equipped only with a water pistol, I shouldn't try tiger-hunting! I need to be realistic about my own limitations.

There is an obvious and serious omission in the way I have made these two points – this is the need to recognize that all of my work on the passage, whether exegesis or meditation, should be carried out in conscious reliance upon God. For the Puritans, the self-directed preaching that was the form in which they meditated on Scripture, was always to be associated with praying the passage into myself, relying upon the Holy Spirit to enlighten me about its meaning. They saw meditation as the bridge between reading (or hearing) the Bible and prayer:

> Meditation is a middle sort of duty between the word and prayer, and hath respect to both. The word feedeth meditation,

---

11   William Perkins, *The Art of Prophesying*, (Edinburgh: Banner of Truth, 1996 [1592]), p. 74.

and meditation feedeth prayer; we must hear that we be not erroneous, and meditate that we be not barren. These duties must always go hand in hand; meditation must follow hearing and precede prayer.[12]

Meditation is the best beginning of prayer, and prayer is the best conclusion of meditation.[13]

Their approach can help us to guard ourselves against the great danger we noted at the end of Chapter 1 – that of working for God without God. At every stage of our preparation for preaching, we must be faithful in praying for the help and guidance of God.

...the inspirer of the Bible is also the illuminator of the Bible's readers and the Bible's hearers, and the empowerer of the Bible's preachers...The whole process of preparation must therefore be prayed through and carried out in conscious dependence on God.[14]

GOT IT?

i.   What is the right context in which my preparation should be done?

ii. What kind of workspace is best for doing my preparation?

iii. How do I break open a passage and get at its meaning?

iv. What is wrong with using commentaries at the beginning of my preparation?

v.   Why is the *digesting* stage of the process so important?

---

[12]   Thomas Manton (1620-1677), quoted in Joel R. Beeke, *Puritan Reformed Spirituality* (Grand Rapids: Reformation Heritage, 2004), p. 79.
[13]   George Swinnock (1627-1673), quoted in Joel R. Beeke, *Puritan Reformed Spirituality*, p. 87.
[14]   David Jackman in William Philip [ed.], *The Practical Preacher*, p. 72.

4. Designing

4.1. Designing: To get you thinking...

Preparing...is important for the beginner, though the more you grow in maturity, the more you can rely on the prompting of the Spirit. I still have the last sermon notes I ever wrote:

> Sunday evening, Third after Trinity, 1995
> 1. Open the Bible, and read a few chapters.
> 2. Glare at the congregation.
> 3. Wait for inspiration.
> (If in doubt, go back to 1, and try again.)

Rev'd Gerald Ambulance, My Ministry Manual, p. 29.

...when you have a clergyman in your family you must accommodate your tastes. I did that very early. When I married Humphrey I made up my mind to like sermons, and I set out by liking the end very much. That soon spread to the middle and the beginning, because I couldn't have the end without them.

George Eliot, *Middlemarch*, (Penguin Classics), (London: Penguin, 1994 [1871-2]), p. 325.

...flinging the already written pages of the Election Sermon into the fire, he forthwith began another, which he wrote with such an impulsive flow of thought and emotion, that he fancied himself inspired; and only wondered that Heaven should see fit to transmit the grand and solemn music of its oracles through so foul an organ-pipe as he. However, leaving that mystery to solve itself, or to go unsolved for ever, he drove his task onward, with earnest haste and ecstasy. Thus the night fled away...morning came, and peeped blushing through the curtains...There he was, with the pen still between his fingers, and a vast, immeasurable tract of written space behind him!

Nathaniel Hawthorne, 'The Scarlet Letter' in William C. Spengemann [ed.], *The Portable Hawthorne*, (Penguin Classics), (New York: Penguin, 2005 [1850]), p. 320f.

...there is an artistic element in a sermon. This is where the labour of preparing sermons comes in. The matter has to be given form, it must be moulded into shape...This involves considerable effort and labour. But someone may ask why all this is necessary. The answer is, because of the people who are going to listen...So you do not take this trouble with the form merely because you believe in 'Art for Art's sake'; the artistic element comes in for the sake of the people, because it helps in the propagation of the Truth and the honour of the Gospel.

Martyn Lloyd-Jones, *Preaching and Preachers*, p. 78-79.

I gladly offer my mouth and heart to your service. I would teach the people and I would continue to learn. To this end I shall meditate diligently on your Word. Use me, dear Lord, as your instrument. Only do not forsake me; for if I were to continue alone, I would quickly ruin everything.

Martin Luther, *Works*, 55 volumes (St Louis: Concordia, 1958-86), 5.123 [1542].

Clarity, logical progression, natural transitions, closely riveted conclusions – these are duties you owe to your hearers. The preacher who stints toil at this point, being disinclined for the strenuous mental discipline involved, is laying upon his congregation the onus of a task which is really his, not theirs. He is transferring to them a burden he ought to have taken on himself.

James S. Stewart, *Heralds of God,* (London: Hodder & Stoughton, 1946), p. 123.

I design plain truth for plain people: therefore, of set purpose, I abstain from all nice and philosophical speculations; from all perplexed and intricate reasonings; and, as far as possible, from even the show of learning...I labour to avoid all words which are not easy to be understood, all which are not used in common life; and, in particular, those kinds of technical terms that so frequently occur in Bodies of Divinity; those modes of speaking which men of reading are intimately acquainted with, but which to common people are an unknown tongue.

John Wesley, *Sermons on Several Occasions,* First Series (London: Epworth, 1944 [1746-60]), p. v.

4.2.   *Designing: Guidance from Scripture*

Do your best to present yourself to God as one approved, a worker who does not need to be ashamed and who correctly handles the word of truth.

2 Timothy 2:15.

A newly inducted minister boasted to his elders that all the time he needed to prepare his sermon was the few minutes it took him to walk to the church from the manse next door. The elders immediately went out and bought a new manse ten kilometres away! They obviously had a much better sense than their preacher did of just how much work needs to go into a good Bible talk.

In the previous session we worked our way through the first two stages of the process of preparation: *discovering* and *digesting*. This would be a good time to refresh your memory about what these stages involve and why they matter, before we consider the next stage in the process.

This *third stage* in the process of preparation is where I turn the fruits of the previous stages – all the notes and ideas from my exegesis of the passage and my subsequent mulling it over – into the Bible talk I will preach. How do I do this?

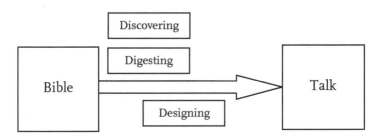

The most helpful way of understanding what I need to do in this *designing* stage is to think of it as a sequence of *five* steps.

   i.   I develop an *outline* for the talk.

   ii.   I decide the *contents* of each point in my outline.

  iii.   I decide how to *end* the talk.

  iv.   I decide how to *begin* the talk.

   v.   I check to see that the talk is *an integrated whole*.

4.3. Designing the Outline

This is the 'S' part of the 'PEST Test' – in order to communicate effectively, my sermon should be *structured*.

4.3.1. Refresher: Why do my hearers need my talks to have a structure?

In simple terms, giving a talk a structure means giving it a *beginning*, a *middle*, and an *ending*. The place to start is in the middle, because this is the heart of the talk. This is where I unpack the message of my passage, and it is this element of the talk that needs a good outline. Why are the beginning and ending of the talk left until later? For the simple reason that I don't know the best way to begin and end the talk until I have a clear idea of what it is going to say!

Before we go any further into this chapter, I need to give you a warning. In developing an outline for my talk on Matthew 6, I am going to take you through a process that might seem unnecessarily fussy and complicated. You might well find yourself wondering whether we really need to bother with what I will be doing with you. Can I ask you to be patient and come with me anyway? Once we have finished developing the outline, I will do my best to deal with any concerns you have about the process involved.

What am I aiming at here? What does my outline need to do? First and foremost, it needs to do justice to the passage I will be expounding! So we are now going to develop an outline for a talk on our sample passage, Matthew 6:5-13.

Turn back to pages 61-62. What does the layout of the 'third step' diagram tell me about the message of this passage? How could I summarize it simply, in a way that gives me an outline I could preach from? Perhaps I will end up with an outline like this:

1. There are *wrong* ways of praying (vv. 5-8)

    a. There is the wrong praying of the hypocrites (vv. 5-6)

    b. There is the wrong praying of the pagans (vv. 7-8)

2. There is a *right* way of praying (vv. 9-13)

At this point I need to ask myself two questions. They are important because they remind me of what I am supposed to be doing here – namely, preparing to communicate God's Word to a group of people.

As we learned in Chapter 2, this means that I need to focus carefully on both *content* and *contact*. The first question is the *content* question: Does the outline summarize the passage accurately? (How might the outline be improved in this regard?) The second question is the *contact* question: Does this outline enable me to make effective contact with the hearers? How could I change it, to make it more effective for this purpose?

I think there is an obvious defect with the outline when it is considered from the *contact* perspective. It *describes* truths for the hearers, but it doesn't *apply* these truths to them. It leaves the message of the passage 'out there', as a set of abstract ideas rather than a Word from the Lord. In fact, although it does a reasonable job of summarizing the passage, it fails to do it justice in one very important respect – it doesn't have the same character as the passage. Jesus is warning and exhorting his disciples about how they pray, not giving them information about various kinds of prayer.

> It takes more than just stating main points...to make an outline truly applicational. True application calls our listeners to respond to the Word, and it is your job to make that response clear to your audience...Simply move the wording of your points out of the indicative mood (the way things are) and into the imperative (a call to the way they should be).[1]

So perhaps I could reword the outline like this:

1. Don't pray the *wrong* way! (vv. 5-8)

    a. Don't try to impress other people (vv. 5-6)

    b. Don't try to impress God (vv. 7-8)

2. Pray the *right* way! (vv. 9-13)

How adequate is this revised outline? Does it achieve the *contact* aim? What are the ways in which it does this? What are some ways in which it doesn't do this sufficiently, or doesn't do it at all? One of its obvious shortcomings is that it doesn't indicate what the right way of praying involves. So I could modify the outline in the following way:

---

[1]   Michael Fabarez, *Preaching That Changes Lives*, (Nashville: Thomas Nelson, 2002), p. 63.

1.   Don't pray the *wrong* way! (vv. 5-8)

    a. Don't try to impress other people (vv. 5-6)

    b. Don't try to impress God (vv. 7-8)

2.   Pray the *right* way! (vv. 9-13)

    a. Remember who God is (v. 9a)

    b. Remember what matters most (vv. 9b-10)

    c. Remember what we really need (vv. 11-13)

Again, from a *contact* perspective, there is an obvious defect with this outline. It is a seven-point talk! The great majority of listeners will struggle to remember that many points, even if the points are obviously based directly on what the passage says – and even if they are worded simply. Only the most gifted preachers can get away with talks that have more than four points at most. At this point in the process, therefore, I have a choice to make. My first option is to eliminate some of the points, so that the talk ends up being tighter and more focused and thus easier for people to follow and to remember later. My second option is to turn the outline into two talks. (If this talk is part of a series, then the second option is probably not open to me.) One way of turning the outline into two talks would be like this:

Talk 1: *Don't pray the wrong way!*

1.   Don't try to impress other people (vv. 5-6).
    → because we are praying to our Father

2.   Don't try to impress God (vv. 7-8).
    → because we are praying to our Father

Talk 2: *Pray the right way!*

1.   Remember who God is (v. 9a)
2.   Remember what matters most (vv. 9b-10)
3.   Remember what we really need (vv. 11-13)

At this point, I might think of another way of wording the outline of the second talk. *I must make sure I write it down* – I don't want to throw away (or forget) *any* ideas at this stage! Later on, I can make a final decision about which is the better outline. The alternative outline might be something like this:

Pray the right way!

1.   Pray *to* God (v. 9a)
2.   Pray *for* God (vv. 9b-10)
3.   Pray for *us* (vv. 11-13)

The advantage of preaching through the passage this way is that there are no more than three main points in either of the talks. The disadvantage is that the second talk could end up with eight sub-points! The first point will need to consider what it means for God to be (a) our Father, and (b) in heaven. The second will need to look at God's name, kingdom, and will. The third will have to say something about each of our daily bread, forgiveness, and protection.

Once I have seen this, I might decide that I really need four talks to cover the passage properly, because the second needs to be split into three. My outlines for these three talks would then be:

Talk 2: *Praying to the real God*

1.   What does it mean to pray to 'our Father'?
2.   What does it mean to pray to the Father 'in heaven'?

Talk 3: *Praying for God*

1.   We pray about God's name
2.   We pray about God's kingdom
3.   We pray about God's will

Talk 4: *Praying for ourselves*

1.   We pray for our bread
2.   We pray to be forgiven
3.   We pray for protection

As I take another look at the outlines, I realize that (at least for talks 3 and 4) I have forgotten the *contact* focus: my points just make statements. So I decide to follow the format of talk 2, and turn each set of three points into *questions*: Why do we pray about the honouring of God's name? Why do we pray about the coming of God's Kingdom? – and so on. Can you think of other ways of making the points more helpful for the hearers?

This is the right place to introduce another really important issue to do with my talk outlines. If I am expounding God's Word, then I will obviously believe that what I preach matters – not because I am preaching it, but because every human being needs to hear, understand,

and respond rightly to the Word of God. If that is so, then it will be worthwhile for people to hear my Bible expositions – yes, even my very faulty efforts. And if it is worth their while to *hear* them, then surely it will be a great help to them if they can also *remember* them afterwards. In which case, I will serve them by working hard, not only at understanding and explaining and applying a passage, but also at wording my talk, especially its main points, in ways that are easy to remember. Our motto is 'if it's worth saying, it's worth remembering!' So is there another way of wording the points that would make the outlines easier for people to remember? If they can remember the outline, then they can take the talk home with them, and it can keep on having an impact in their lives. Can you think of a way to make the points more memorable?

If no inspiration strikes now, it's a good idea to come back to this after I have done the rest of my preparation. But before we can move on, we must resolve the question of how many talks we will take to cover this passage. Let us suppose that the choice is not ours, and that we will have to deal with the passage in just one talk. How are we going to do so? It seems a shame to have had so many good ideas about what we could do and to be unable to use all of them. So how do we decide which ones we can and will use? As soon as we reach this question, we face several dangers.

The first is that we will try to cram everything into the talk somehow because we are unwilling to sacrifice any of the good ideas we had to work hard for. This is where we need to remember the PEST Test, and the importance of our preaching being Plain – that is, clear and easy to follow. In Chapter 2 we saw that preparing plain preaching involves pruning – that is, leaving out everything that will prevent the hearers from grasping the main message of the passage. My pruning-shears are especially needed when I have had lots of good ideas, because some of them must go if my talk is not going to be impossibly crowded and overloaded.

The second danger facing us at this point is that we will make our choices about what to say and what to omit for the wrong reasons. Out of all the ideas I have had, there might be one approach that appeals to me more than the others. But in expository preaching the passage and not the preacher is in control of the content and direction of the talk. The right way to decide what to include and what to omit is to ask these two questions: What is the 'big idea' of the passage? And what is the passage doing with this big idea? Now, what conclusions about my talk do I reach by asking these two questions?

The passage's 'big idea' is fairly obvious – it is all about 'how disciples of Jesus should pray'. What it is doing with this idea is warning against two wrong approaches to prayer and also teaching the right approach. I want to make sure that I have understood this rightly, so I check to see how the context of the passage helps me. I discover that the passages just before and just after this one have the same basic shape as the passage on prayer (6:2-4, 16-18). They begin by warning against wrong approaches (to giving, and to fasting), and then go on to teach the right approach. In both cases the right approach is based on the fact that God is our Father and he sees what is unseen by others (verses 4, 18). This contrast between the two approaches, and the reason why the second is right, is exactly what we find in our passage – so this must determine the focus and thrust of my talk. Everything that doesn't fit will have to go – not into the bin, but into my ideas file, for possible use on another occasion. Once this is clear to me, I realize that the best outline for my talk is this one:

Major point 1: *Don't pray the wrong way!*

1. Don't try to impress other people (vv. 5-6).
   → because we are praying to our Father

2. Don't try to impress God (vv. 7-8).
   → because we are praying to our Father

Major point 2: *Pray the right way!*

1. Remember who God is (v. 9a)
2. Remember what matters most (vv. 9b-10)
3. Remember what we really need (vv. 11-13)

Am I ready now to move on, to fill in the outline I have decided on? Only if I am really clear about the primary focus and major thrust of the talk. I realize that I have not got this as clear as I need to, so that my talk runs the risk of sounding like two talks thrown together, like two ferrets jostling in a sack. So I need to go back to the passage again, and to ask what is its core truth, its beating heart, the hub that binds all of the individual spokes together?'

As I read the passage again, and then look through the draft outlines in which I tried to capture what it is saying, I find that the answer is clear and simple. The essential truth underlying everything else in the passage is conveyed by the words, 'Our Father in heaven'. It is failing to respond to and rely on this God that makes wrong prayer wrong (verses 5-8). It is relating to this God and recognizing that this is who he is that makes right prayer right (verses 9-13). Everything in the passage either leads up to these words or follows on from them; this is its key. So this must provide my talk with its focus and aim; this is what I will keep on emphasizing throughout the talk – so what I need now is a clear, simple, easily remembered way of stating the two truths that God is our 'Father' and that he is 'in heaven'. How can I do this?

In the *discovering* stage of my preparation, I learned that 'in heaven' is not the Bible's way of saying that God is a long way away, like an absentee landlord. Rather, it is a biblical way of telling us that God is supreme and sovereign (see, for example, 2 Chronicles 20:6; Psalm 115:3). This means that a 'Father in heaven' is a sovereign Father, a Father who rules over everything. In light of this, I could state the two main points this way: God is (1) our *Father* and (2) our *King*. This is certainly clear, simple, and easy to remember – but is there an even better way of saying it? One possibility is to look for keywords that sound the same, because this is one of the most powerful aids to memory. So it occurs to me that I could restate this twofold affirmation as: God is (1) our *Father* and (2) our *Ruler*. Because both of the keywords have two syllables and end with the same sound, my hearers will hear them as a matching pair. This makes it more likely that they will be able to remember them. Other ways of achieving the same outcome would be to replace the nouns with verbs or adjectives – so my wording could be:

Our God is (1) *merciful* and (2) *powerful.*

Our God is (1) *merciful* and (2) *mighty.*

Our God (1) *cares* and (2) *controls.*

Our God is (1) *good* and (2) *great.*

The last of these is the simplest – but its obvious disadvantage is that it doesn't use Jesus' own words, especially the key word, 'Father'. So perhaps we can combine it with our previous attempt, to give us: God is (1) a good Father and (2) a great Ruler. We don't have to jettison the other possibilities, because we can use them throughout the talk in *explaining* and *summarising* this fundamental point.

Once I reach this point I realize that 'Ruler' sounds just a bit too abstract to me, even a bit olde-worlde. Yet if I keep it, I can also keep using the key word, 'Father'. So although I feel that it isn't ideal, I decide that this is the best option for stating this crucial point – but alongside it, I also plan to use the much simpler formula, 'God is good, and God is great'. This is what I want people to go home saying to themselves; this is what I want to motivate and guide them as they come to pray – because this is what I am now convinced is the key to this whole passage.

> Phrase with special care, and repeat at intervals, whatever you wish the hearer to remember. Do not expect him to remember everything, but take pains that he will remember something.[2]

To take one more example: How could I change the outline of *Talk 4*, which is now the third part of my second major point? I could express it this way:

We need (1) food   (2) forgiveness   and   (3) protection.

It would be much better for the hearers if all three points sounded similar. But try as I might, I can't think of a word starting with 'f' that fits the third point. So could I find suitable 'p' words for the other two points? That turns out to be quite easy.

We need (1) provisions   (2) pardon   and   (3) protection.

That works OK but then I find myself being a little uneasy about the fact that the points don't explicitly acknowledge God. It occurs to me that one way of making it very clear that the passage is about *prayer* is to turn the points around. Instead of talking about what we need, why not talk about what God gives? So I could express the points in either of the following ways:

God is (1) our provider   (2) our pardoner   and   (3) our protector.

God   (1) provides   (2) pardons   and   (3) protects.

But now I'm just stating ideas, even though they are great ideas! I am telling my hearers something, rather than calling them to something. So perhaps I should express the points like this:

I should ask God:

(1) to provide for me   (2) to pardon me   (3) to protect me.

---

[2]   Andrew W. Blackwood, *Expository Preaching for Today*, (Grand Rapids: Baker, 1943), p. 92-94.

Once more: why am I doing this? Not to play word games, and kid myself that I'm working! I owe it to my hearers to make the structure of my talk as easy as possible to understand while I am preaching it, and as easy as possible to recall afterwards. The more I work at doing this, the better I will get. It may not come easily to begin with, but if I persevere, it will gradually become less difficult.

Where have we got to? I am not any longer planning to cover this passage in two, three, or four talks but in one. This will mean that I will have to leave out quite a bit, but how much? Will I have to leave out all the good ideas I had about the contents of the Lord's Prayer, for example? Then it occurs to me that this is where the work I have done already can prove its worth. I don't have to exclude everything, because all I will have time to do with most of the sub-points is just to state them. If I do so in a way that makes them easy to understand and easy to remember that will be a great help to the hearers even if that is all I give them. For example, when I get to the last section of the prayer (verses 11-13), I might just say,

> In the second half of his prayer, Jesus teaches us that we should ask God for what we really need.
>
> *Give us today our daily bread* – we should ask him for our daily bread, because he is a Father who *provides* for his children.
>
> *Forgive us our debts as we also have forgiven our debtors* – we should ask him to forgive us, because he is a Father who *pardons* his children.
>
> *And lead us not into temptation but deliver us from evil* – we should ask him to save us from temptation and evil because he is a Father who *protects* his children.
>
> We pray with confidence because we pray to our Father in heaven. Because he is good (he is our Father), and because he is great (he is in heaven), he generously provides, and mercifully pardons, and powerfully protects.

And now I am ready to leave the task of developing an *outline,* and move on to the next stage. But first, I have a promise to keep. You will recall that I made a commitment before we began developing the talk outline. I said that once we had done so I would consider your unease about whether we really needed to go through such a complex and fussy process in order to arrive at an outline for our talk. So why have we done what we just did?

There are two reasons for taking so much trouble over the points in my talk outline. The first has to do with the 'S' in the PEST-Test. My talks need to be structured so that the hearers can come with me on the step-by-step journey through my talk. This is why the points in my outline are like the rungs of a ladder or the stepping-stones I use to cross a creek. But this is where your objections begin. You have no problem accepting that there must be a talk outline, but you can't see why it is necessary to spend so much time getting the points to fit together so tightly. As long as they are both true to the passage and clear and simple, why is this not good enough?

This brings us to the second reason for making such an effort to get the points right. This is our principle, 'If it's worth saying, it's worth remembering!' We want the talk to go on doing good to the hearers after they have heard it. But if this is going to happen, they must be able to remember what the talk said about the passage. They will do so only if we make the main points in the talk as easy as possible to remember. The best way of doing this is to word the points in such a way that they fit together and form a united group. And the best way of achieving this kind of cohesion is for the points to share a common structure and sound-pattern. I'm most likely to recall points that sound similar, similar enough for me to 'see' them as a natural grouping.

This brings me to one last thing that I need to say about developing a talk outline. If you still find my way of doing it unnatural, and can't really see yourself doing the same, then I have a challenge for you. It is this: use another method of achieving the same goals. That is, find a way that is more natural for you, but a way that will enable your hearers to come with you through the talk and then to recall its main points in the hours and days after they hear it, so that they can go on benefiting from it. The fundamental issue is this: my *ministry of the Word* means that I am committed to a *ministry of words*. I must work hard to find the best possible words for conveying the message of the Bible, so that my hearers will understand it, and remember it, and be grasped by it.

4.4. *Designing the Contents*

This is the second of the five steps in the *designing* process. How do I do this? What should the contents do? They will *explain*, *support*, and *apply* the points in my outline. They *explain* by making clear the meaning of what the passage teaches. They *support* by giving reasons for believing what the passage teaches. They *apply* by showing the implications of what the passage teaches, and urging the hearers to take this teaching in and live it out.

My first responsibility to my hearers is to give an *explanation* of each point in the outline. If my outline is an accurate summary of the passage, this is another way of saying that I need to explain the meaning of each major point the passage is making. There needs to be enough explanation of each point to make the meaning clear, but not so much that it gets swamped. And only the main points need to be explained – I cannot explain everything in one Bible talk. And if I need to explain the explanations, then it's high time I got out my pruning shears!

Some preachers regularly explain what is in the passage by referring to passages elsewhere in the Bible. In my opinion, this is of doubtful value, for two reasons. The first is that it distracts the hearers from the passage to which they are meant to be responding. The second is that it can easily give the impression that only those who know everything in the Bible (like the preacher!) can understand anything in the Bible. There will be some occasions when the best explanation *will* come from elsewhere in the Bible. I am not arguing that this should never be done, but protesting against a tendency to do this most of the time.

One of the most helpful ways of explaining something is to compare or contrast it with something else. A comparison or analogy is almost always an effective way of communicating – 'The Kingdom of God is like...' Likewise, if I enable the hearers to see what something *isn't*, this can help them to see what it is. So, in speaking about the Lord's Prayer and the difference between it and the two wrong ways of praying that are ruled out by Jesus, I might say something like this:

> But what is it that makes this way of praying right? Is it that the people praying have no trace of hypocrisy about them, unlike those in verse 5? No, this can't be it, because the disciples Jesus is speaking to are far from perfect – just like us!
>
> Then does right prayer mean that those praying abandon the use of words – unlike those in verse 7, who have a great deal to say when they pray? This can't be right either, because Jesus gives us words to use when we pray.

Then is right prayer praying that is done in a special place? Or praying that is done in a particular way, with special preparation or special actions or special equipment? No, this can't be right either, because Jesus never told his disciples about any of these things.

It is the content that makes this prayer right – it is right because of who it is addressed to and what it asks him to be and to do. Have another look at it with me...

Can you think of another way of doing this that would be more natural for you?

The task of explanation overlaps with that of *illustration*. Illustrating the message means shedding light on it: that is, enabling the hearers to see it more clearly. This involves depicting each idea in a way that highlights its essential features. How can I do this? It is quite common to think that illustrations need to be stories. Yet while it is true that an anecdote can often be a helpful illustration, the use of vivid pictorial language is often just as effective. Either way, the illustration will be a brief snapshot of something we all experience or at least know about; it provides a 'for instance' that everyone can relate to.

It is important to remember that my illustrations must be servants, not masters; their only job is to help the hearers to get the message. If finding illustrations takes too much time in my preparation, or if they take up too much time in my preaching, then my illustrations have become too big for their boots.

> ...sermon illustrations unleash the audience's imagination. The listeners use your spoken words to draw pictures in their minds. Because of the power of the human imagination, you need to ask, 'What specifically do I want them thinking about and imagining as I present the truth about God?'[3]

> Don't punch people with a raw idea; shake their hands with an example...Good examples are worth thousands of words.[4]

> A powerful way to make your sermon memorable and picturesque is to use analogies like Jesus did...An analogy is a

---

[3]   Terry G. Carter, J. Scott Duvall, J. Daniel Hays, *Preaching God's Word*, p. 144f.
[4]   James Rye, *The Communicator's Craft*, p. 52-53.

one-line illustration, a porthole of light illuminating your message and pegging it to your listener's memory.[5]

How can we illustrate our talk on Matthew 6:5-13? We have already decided to emphasize that right praying is based on the twin facts that God is good (our Father) and God is great (our Ruler). For this to be clear to our hearers, they will need to grasp what it means to say that God is 'in heaven'. We can explain what this means by illustrating it – and we can illustrate it by appealing to the hearers' imagination. We might say something like this:

> What do you think of when you say that God is 'in heaven'?
>
> Do you imagine heaven as something like a palace, with the throne-room decked out in gold and marble, so that the whole thing sparkles, and stuns with its beauty? And God is there, majestic and magnificent in appearance?
>
> Or do you find it hard to imagine what heaven is like – so that, in the end, you see it as full of absences? You can only imagine it by focusing on what isn't there, on what it isn't like? So you see God as a blank, something like a ghost, but huge – much, much bigger than any ordinary ghost?
>
> Or do you find that you can't see anything when you think of heaven? But whatever it is like, you think of it as somewhere else? So to say that God is 'in heaven' means that he isn't here; he is not in our territory but in his?
>
> So it might come as a relief to you to discover that the Bible has something very different in mind when it tells us that God is 'in heaven'. Listen to how one of Israel's kings began his prayer to God... (2 Chronicles 20:6).
>
> Do you see what he is saying? For God to be in heaven does not mean that he is a long way away, busy in his own domain.
>
> Instead it means that he is mighty and powerful: *power and might are in your hand.*
>
> It means that he is involved in this world as its King: *you rule over all the kingdoms of the nations.*

---

[5] Hershael W. York & Bert Decker, *Preaching with BOLD Assurance*, p. 161.

It means that he is not a distant God but a sovereign God. No one can defeat him or prevent him from doing what he decides to do: *no one can withstand you.* As we read in Psalm 115:3, *Our God is in heaven; he does whatever pleases him.*

So for God to be 'in heaven' means that he is a great Ruler, a mighty King. The whole world is under his control; he rules over all.

Can you think of another way of doing this that would be more natural for you?

My talk might need to provide a *justification* of one or more of the main points. This is where I show why it is to be accepted and believed. This means anticipating any unease the hearers might have and making a case for what they might otherwise struggle to accept. My task here is overcoming barriers, removing the roadblocks that would keep the truth from reaching the hearers. Unless the point concerned is the main point of the talk, I will do this quite briefly.

For our talk on Matthew 6:5-13, let us suppose that we have decided that the point we have just made needs some justification. We know that the idea of absolute power has very negative 'vibes' for some of our hearers. So we might deal with this issue as follows:

It is true that supreme power can be a terrible thing. We only have to mention the names Hitler, Stalin, Pol Pot, Saddam Hussein and Robert Mugabe to realize how evil such power can be. In the wrong hands, supreme power has hounded millions into poverty and misery and cruel deaths.

But what if supreme power was in good hands? That would be a very different story, wouldn't it? Such power would no longer be something to fear; instead, we would welcome it and rejoice over it. And this is exactly what we find in God: supreme power married to absolute goodness; mercy and might coupled together; sovereign greatness and saving grace joined unbreakably and eternally.

We are right to be troubled at the prospect of supreme power in human hands – but when it is in God's hands, it gives us confidence to come to him and to ask him for what we need. When there is no limit to his power and no limit to his love, there need be no limits to what we ask or how often we come. Supreme power in the wrong hands? Frightening! Supreme power in good hands, in God's hands? Faith-building!

Can you think of another way of doing this that would be more natural for you?

Finally, my talk will also include application of each of the main points. There are two important questions to ask about this: How do I work out the application? Where do I put it in the talk?

The answer to the first question is simple and straightforward: I work out the application by working out *why* the passage says what it says. When I know how the passage was meant to impact its original audience, then I know what impact my talk should have on me and my hearers.

> Effective application is an outgrowth of the purpose of the text. Every passage or literary unit of Scripture has an intention, an objective, and a purpose. Every passage of Scripture is aiming at...some desired change in the thinking, attitude, and behavior of the readers. Our job, as expositors, is to determine through the exegetical study of the text what the purpose is. During our study we must ask ourselves, why is this portion of Scripture here?[6]

When I come to translate the general aim of the talk (which reflects the purpose of the passage) into specific applications, I need to strike a balance. On the one hand, I must not state the application so generally that it lacks teeth. If it is too vague, too abstract, or too predictable, nobody will think that it applies to anybody. On the other hand, I must not state the application in such specific terms that it relates to only a few of the hearers. If it is too narrow or too pointed everybody will assume that it is meant for somebody else! And I must not draw out so many applications that the hearers are overwhelmed.

It is worth noting here that just as *Illustration* overlaps with the task of *Explanation*, it also overlaps with that of *Application*. And just as the need for *Justification* can arise out of our *Explanation*, so its contents can lead into the *Application*. This is just a reminder not to approach these tasks in a wooden manner, as though every point in our talk had

---

[6] Winfred Omar Neely in John Koessler [ed.], *The Moody Handbook of Preaching*, (Chicago: Moody, 2008), p. 58f.

to have *Explanation*, then *Illustration*, next *Justification*, and finally *Application*. Instead, we should do with each point what will prove most beneficial to the hearers – *Explanation* where the meaning is unclear to them; *Justification* where the meaning is clear but troubling; and so on.

> Illustrations bridge the gap between explanation and application. Some make the thought clearer; others help us picture ourselves obeying it; but all good illustrations move us toward the intended response. Illustrations make truth concrete and personal by giving a 'for instance.'[7]

The answer to our second question is also simple, but not straightforward. Where the application section(s) comes in the talk depends on the way the talk deals with the passage. In some cases, the application should come at the end of each section of the talk. To say this in another way, each main point in the talk will have its application spelled out before I move to the next point. In other cases, the application will be saved up until the end: the conclusion will also be the application. There are even some cases in which the application could come first, in the introduction. (It will then need to be repeated, perhaps at the end of each section of the talk, but certainly in the conclusion.)

> Instead of saying throughout the sermon, 'This is what God said to the Israelites,' and then, at the very end, asking, 'Now what does all this mean to us today?' the preacher from the outset ought to tell his people, 'This is what God says to *you*. How do we know this? Well, listen to what he told the Israelites, who were facing circumstances not altogether unlike our own...'[8]

> Application finishes the sermon. It calls for response and action after the truth of God's Word has been presented. Without application the sermon is incomplete...Application begins with a proper understanding of the meaning of the text...The makeup and character of the audience determine the specifics of your application.[9]

---

7   Greg Scharf, *Prepared to Preach,* (Fearn: Mentor, 2005), p. 140f.
8   Jay E. Adams, *Truth Apparent,* p. 78f.
9   Terry G. Carter, J. Scott Duvall, J. Daniel Hays, *Preaching God's Word,* (Grand Rapids: Zondervan, 2005), p. 130.

4.5. Designing the Conclusion

This is the third step in the *designing* process. The first and most important thing to say about this is that I *must* do it!

> Pilots have long joked that flying is really hours of boredom punctuated by moments of sheer terror...The tough parts are...the takeoff and the landing. Those actions require more skill, more concentration, and more attention than any other part of piloting an airplane. Preaching is similar.[10]

Many good talks have been spoiled because their preachers had not prepared a conclusion. Instead, when they reached the end of what they had prepared, they kept talking in the hope that a suitable ending would come to them eventually. Almost always, it doesn't! And when it does, the reason is that God is having mercy on the hearers!

It is not accidental that the expressions 'famous last words' and 'her dying wish' are well known, because the fact is that final words do carry weight. Just because they are the last to be uttered, they linger. Similarly, we want the final words of the talk to hit home and leave their mark.

4.5.1. What should the conclusion do?

It should get the hearers to look back and to look forward. It should answer two basic questions:

i. 'Where have we been?' It will remind the hearers of the main points in the talk.

ii. 'Where do we go from here?' It presses home the application, so that the message of the passage has its appropriate impact on the hearers.

4.5.2. How can this be done?

It cannot be done with 'lettuce'! General exhortations, like 'let us pray more' or 'let us determine to be more this, or less that', have about as much impact on the hearers as pounding them over the head with a

---

[10] Hershael W. York & Bert Decker, *Preaching with BOLD Assurance*, p. 174.

lettuce leaf. Lettuce not end our talks this way!

- Because it needs to fit the point of the passage and the theme of the talk, the conclusion will not always follow the same pattern.

- The conclusion might be a set of questions: 'What changes are you going to make so that you respond to what God says to us in this passage? Where will you begin? Will it be in your relationship with someone that you live with? Or someone that you work with? Will you begin today? How will you do it?'

- It might be a direct challenge: 'Now you know what God wants, so make sure you give it to him today. Why not do it now?' Or, 'Now you know what God has promised to do for you, don't miss out: take hold of it today.'

- It might be a brief story that drives the point of the passage home.

- It might pick up something that was raised but deliberately not resolved in the introduction, and repeat it in a way that is striking and challenging.

> Do not approach the landing field three or four times, only to soar up into the blue again at the last second. Instead, when the congregation has been alerted to fasten seat belts (by a 'finally' or some similar signal) bring her in for a full flap landing on the first approach.[11]

> If the beginning of a sermon is crucial because it determines whether people will listen to us or not, the ending is equally critical because it affects what they will do with what they have heard...So the preacher has to ask...the question: 'What do I want this sermon to do?', not 'What do I want this sermon to say?'[12]

> ...possibly the commonest reason for weak endings is the most serious. We have no strong conclusion because we had no clearly defined aim...Like a car without brakes, a sermon with no end in view can come to a stop only by loss

---

[11] Jay E. Adams, *Pulpit Speech*, (P & R, 1971), p. 56f.
[12] Simon Coupland, *Stripping Preaching to its Bare Essentials*, (Oxford: Monarch, 2005), p. 87.

of momentum.[13]

How should we finish our Lord's Prayer talk? We will want to state the main points again, because we want people to be able to remember them and go on considering them and benefiting from them in the days and weeks to come. Then we will zero in on the major focus of the talk, which we drew from the passage in the *discovery* stage of our preparation. We want people to keep reminding themselves that the God to whom we belong and to whom we pray is a good Father and a great Ruler. So our final words might be along these lines:

> If you are anything like me, your biggest problem is not wrong prayer but non-prayer! You don't really pray like the hypocrites or the pagans; in fact, you don't really pray like anyone, for you don't pray very much at all.

> Could this be the solution to our problem? Has the Lord Jesus gone right to the heart of our failure? Do we need to remind ourselves that the God we belong to is a good Father and a great Ruler, that he is mighty and merciful, that he has us in his care and the world under his control?

> Will you take this to heart today? Will you make time today to come to God? Will you tell him that you come to him with confidence because of who he is: our good Father and our great Ruler? Will you tell him that you can see now that you can depend on him in every situation? Will you then tell him what you need, what those closest to you need, what you know about the needs of others?

> And then, will you take this with you into tomorrow? Whenever things don't go according to plan, will you tell yourself that God is good and God is great? And then will you say so to him?

> This isn't rocket science, is it? The key to right praying is knowing who God is – and we do know who he is; we know what he is like. We know we can depend on him, so let's do it!

Can you think of another way of doing this that would be more natural for you?

---

[13]   R. E. O. White, *A Guide to Preaching*, p. 107.

4.5.3. *Who has the last word?*

What happens in most churches when the preacher has reached the last full stop in his sermon? In the very next breath he will say, 'Lettuce spray', and will then lead the congregation in prayer. *The time has come to question this tradition!*

There are two very good reasons for discontinuing this practice. The first has to do with me as the *preacher*. I have worked hard on the talk, putting a lot of thought and prayer and time into it. I have prepared every part of the talk, because I know that it is foolish to rely upon the inspiration of the moment to come up with the best way of explaining and applying the passage. And then, right at the point where my carefully thought-out conclusion should be going to work on the hearers, I stifle its impact by launching into an impromptu prayer! There is a double irony about this: in the first place, it is the only part of the preaching event that I have not prepared, and secondly, because I haven't prepared it, my prayer will usually be a repeat of the talk's conclusion: I will repeat the main points and the application, but this time to God instead of to the hearers (who now get it for the second time, of course).

The second reason for abandoning this practice has to do with my *hearers*. If they have accompanied me on the journey through the passage, and recognized afresh God's grace or God's claim on their lives, what will they want to do at the conclusion of the talk? If they have been receptive during the talk, they will want to be responsive after it: that is, they will want to do business with God. But they then face a double frustration. The first is that I prevent them from praying by doing it for them. The second is that my prayer is (a) not what they would have prayed, and (b) a re-run of the last bit of the talk.

Then what should we do at the end of the talk? Nothing! If I have ended it in a suitably challenging way, then I should allow people a minute or two to reflect on, take in, and pray over what I have said. If I think they won't know what to do with silence, after I have finished the talk I could say something like this: 'We have heard God's Word and thought about its implications for our lives. Now we will spend a few moments in silence so that each of us can take hold of what God has been saying to us.' Better still, I could get the leader of the service to say this – but it needs to be done immediately after I have finished speaking.

One last thing: sometimes the best possible way of concluding will be for me to pray! But only sometimes, and only when I myself am so moved by the way the Spirit of God has been working as the Word is preached that I don't have to grope around for something to say in a closing prayer, but find it welling up within me in an almost irresistible way.

4.6. Designing the Introduction

This is the fourth of five steps in the *designing* process. Again, the first thing to be said about this is that I *must* do it! Many a talk that turned out to be good went largely unheard because the preacher tried to think of the opening sentence or two while he was putting his Bible and his notes on the lectern – and the result was the verbal equivalent of the way a dog turns around three or four times while settling down into its sleeping basket!

4.6.1. But since the introduction comes first, why do I prepare it last?

The answer is rather obvious when I think about it: I don't know what the introduction should say until I know what it is introducing. Only when I have worked out what the talk is going to say and do can I work out the best way of introducing it.

4.6.2. What should the introduction do?

It needs to answer two questions the hearer will have:

i.   'Where are you planning to take me?' The introduction serves as an *orientation* for the hearers: it presents *the theme* of the talk. In this sense, the introduction is a *menu*.

ii. 'Why should I come with you?' The introduction provides *motivation*: it gives those present *a reason to listen* to the talk.

From the first words, hearers should expect that something significant is about to happen.[14]

There are three types of preachers: those to whom you cannot listen; those to whom you can listen; and those to

---

[14]   Michael J. Quicke, *360-Degree Preaching*, p. 181.

whom you must listen. During the introduction the congregation usually decides the kind of speaker addressing them...[15]

When working out how to answer these questions in my introduction, I need to remember that, unlike me, the hearers have not spent their week either in the world of the Bible or in the orbit of the church. For the most part, they will not have church questions pressing on them (as I probably do), and they are unlikely to find biblical and theological issues gripping for their own sake (as I am inclined to do). My introduction must show that I take *their* world seriously. Otherwise, they are unlikely to see any good reason for joining me on the journey through the passage.

4.6.3. How can this be done?

The preacher who began his talk like this is not a good model to follow: 'As I understand it, my job is to speak to you and your job is to listen to me – and I'm very much hoping that we both finish at the same time.' So what kind of introduction is most likely to be effective?

It should *not* assume that the hearers are already eager and expectant, focused on what is to come and longing to hear it. So opening sentences like 'You will remember that last Sunday we learned about...' or 'Today we come to Matthew chapter 6' should be avoided like the plague!

It can be a provocative or unexpected question: 'If you knew that you only had two hours left to live, what would you do with them?' It can be a challenging or intriguing statement. It can be an interesting (but brief) anecdote. It can be a striking quotation or statistic. And just occasionally, when it is appropriate, I *might* begin with a joke. (This isn't obligatory, despite widespread tendencies that might suggest otherwise!)

It is the same with men as with donkeys: whoever would hold them fast must get a very good grip on their ears.[16]

An introduction will not arrest your congregation if it doesn't

---

[15] Haddon W. Robinson, *Biblical Preaching*, p. 175.
[16] Russian proverb, quoted in Haddon W. Robinson, *Biblical Preaching*, p. 166.

address the question, 'What difference does all this make?'...the introduction is the place where your applicational thrust begins.[17]

Only the preacher [has] the idea that folk come to church desperately anxious to hear what happened to the Jebusites.[18]

You may be thrilled with the theme of your sermon, but as yet no one else is; so you have to begin where people are and move them on from there...a good introduction compels people to come with you in spite of themselves. It plays the role of the baited hook in fishing.[19]

How will we begin our Lord's Prayer talk? The introduction should get the hearers ready to receive the main point of the talk, which is the key to the passage. Perhaps I could do so like this:

I have a problem with prayer. It's not that I don't understand prayer sufficiently; it's that I don't pray enough.

I can explain this problem in various ways. Sometimes, I justify my lack of prayer by telling myself how little time I have – but somehow, I manage to have enough time for all the things I really want to do – really necessary things, like watching the cricket and the football on TV!

Sometimes, I tell myself that praying seems unreal, because it's talking to an invisible presence. But I have managed perfectly well to cope with other things that seemed unreal until I got to the point where they seemed normal – things like getting used to wearing spectacles.

Sometimes I explain the problem another way – but the trouble is that I know that these are all just excuses.

I get the distinct impression that you know what I am talking about, that I am speaking for you and not just for me. So why do we find prayer so difficult? Why do we find it so hard to be faithful in prayer?

The real issue is very simple – and the Lord Jesus puts his finger

---

[17]   Michael Fabarez, *Preaching That Changes Lives*, p. 102.
[18]   H. E. Fosdick, quoted in Warren W. Wiersbe, *The Dynamics of Preaching*, p. 158.
[19]   Denis Lane, *Preach the Word*, p. 73-74.

right on it in the passage we have just heard. What is he telling us about the secret of true prayer? Look with me at where he begins...

Can you think of another way of doing this that would be more natural for you?

4.7. Checking for Integration

I do this fifth and final step by asking *three important questions*. First, is this talk going somewhere? This is where I look *along* the outline, to check that the talk is making progress towards the goal. Secondly, is all of the talk heading in the same direction? This is where I look *across* the outline, to check that each part of the talk fits into its location and makes its proper contribution. Thirdly, does the direction of the talk properly reflect the main thrust of the passage?

> A good way to think of this is using the clothesline concept. The main thesis statement of the sermon [the 'big idea'] is like a clothesline and the sermon points are the clothes hanging on the line, all connected together and attached to the line. Thus, when writing points, be careful to use words that show the close connection between the points and the thesis statement.[20]

If the talk doesn't hang together, then I need to rework or omit the sections that are not integrated sufficiently with the rest of it. The following samples might be in need of some slight modifications in this connection!

> Corn is a very useful vegetable. If it were not for corn there would be no corn cakes with butter and molasses. Corn grows in large fields, and you can plough it with a horse. There was a man who had a cornfield, and he had no horse, but he had a large and faithful wife, who took care of it, accompanied by a trusty dog, while he wrote poetry for the papers. We ought to be thankful if we have a good wife, which is much better than hanging around saloons and wasting your time in idleness. Corn is also used to feed hogs with, and it can be made into corn cob pipes, which will make you sick if you are not accustomed to it. Let us firmly resolve that we will reform and lead a better life.

---

[20]   Terry G. Carter, J. Scott Duvall, J. Daniel Hays, *Preaching God's Word*, p. 110.

A pig is a funny animal, but it has some uses. Our dog doesn't like pigs. Our dog's name is Nero. Our teacher read a piece one day about a wicked man called Nero. My Dad is a good man. Men are very useful. Men are different from women, and my Mum isn't like my Dad. My Mum says that a ring around the moon means that rain is coming. And that is all I know about pigs.

I have now worked out my outline, worked out the contents of each point, worked out the talk's introduction and conclusion, and checked to see that it all hangs together. Does that mean that I have completed the *designing* stage of my preparation? Maybe! There are two reasons why I might not be ready to move on to the next stage just yet. The first is this: I might need to see if I can find a clearer, simpler, more memorable way of wording the points in the outline. It will often be easier to do this once I have finished working out the talk. Why does this matter?

Refresher: *If it's worth saying, it's worth remembering!...* Here we are following the example of the Teacher, who 'searched to find just the right words, and what he wrote was upright and true.' (Ecclesiastes 12:10)

There is a second reason why I might not be ready to move to the next stage of preparation. My talk might need more work, but I will probably be unaware of its defects right now. It's very hard to be objective about something that I have just spent the last three or four hours struggling to produce! I will see the whole thing more clearly if I can let it lie for another day or so. If I can take more time to let it percolate away at the back of my mind, I am likely to come up with several worthwhile ideas about how I could improve it. So, if it is at all possible, I should now give myself another *digesting* break.

GOT IT?

i.   What should the outline of a talk do?

ii.   What can the content of a talk do with each point in the outline?

iii.   Where does the application come in a talk?

iv.   What should I do at the end of my talk?

v.   Why is the introduction usually the last part of a talk to be prepared?

5. Defining

5.1. Defining: To get you thinking...

If it's a straightforward passage that no one can misunderstand or disagree with, then, in theory, once you've read it the congregation has learned everything it's going to learn and you might as well stop there. In practice, however, that means there'd be no sermon. So you need to fill out your time repeating it in different words...Greek is another good time-killer. Try this kind of thing: 'Now the word translated 'preaching' here is the Greek word *kerygma*. And that comes from the verb *kerysso*, meaning "to preach". So when St Paul says "preaching", what that word really means is "preaching".' Or alternatively: 'The word translated "Spirit" here is the Greek word *pneuma* which means "wind". And that's where we get the term "pneumatic tyres" from. So what St Paul really means when he says "Be filled with the Spirit" is that we should be like the tyres of the Lord, ready to go anywhere for him, adding comfort to his journey through eternity and ever vigilant for the broken glass of the Enemy. Or full of wind, alternatively.'

Rev'd Gerald Ambulance, *My Ministry Manual*, p. 31f.

There is no point in speaking at all if our words are not understood by the people to whose understanding our words are directed. The teacher, then, will avoid all words that do not communicate...

Augustine, *On Christian Teaching*, p. 116.

...that preaching without books' no good, only when a man has a gift, and has the Bible at his fingers' ends...in my youth I've heard the Ranters out o' doors in Yorkshire go on for an hour or two on end, without ever sticking fast a minute...But our parson's no gift at all that way; he can preach as good a sermon as needs be heard when he writes it down. But when he tries to preach wi'out book, he rambles about, and doesn't stick to his text; and every now and then he flounders about like a sheep as has cast itself, and can't get on'ts legs again.

George Eliot, 'The Sad Fortunes of the Reverend Amos Barton' in *Scenes of Clerical Life*, p. 9.

What do our clergy lose by reading their sermons? They lose preaching, the preaching of the voice in many cases, the preaching of the eyes almost always.

J. C. and A. W. Hare, *Guesses at Truth,* (1827).

The *Down-Headed Manuscript Minah* never perches in the pulpit without a sheaf of paper in front of him. And since it is characteristic of this particular preacher bird to read his sermons rather than speak them, he is forced to adopt a characteristic head-down posture on the perch. Consequently, the regular church birds perched in front of him are more familiar with the feathers of his topknot than they are with his face...This preacher bird's worst moment in the pulpit came the morning the platform fan blew all eight pages of his manuscript off the pulpit, scattering seven of them over the communion table, the memorial gift floral arrangement and the front row of perches. But the page he had been reading landed in the baptismal font, mistakenly left uncovered after its last use. It was the first time the congregation had seen his face in the middle of a sermon. They wondered if he always looked that surprised on his second point.

LeRoy Koopman, *Guide to Ecclesiastical Birdwatching,* (Glendale: G/L Publications, 1973), p. 31f.

All preachers should be understood. Preaching is not primarily a fine art. It is a medium for conveying urgent meaning. The man who uses it as a way of displaying his gifts has prostituted his high calling.

W. E. Sangster, *Power in Preaching,* (London: Epworth, 1958), p. 64.

The minister gave out his text and droned along monotonously through an argument that was so prosy that many a head by-and-by began to nod—and yet it was an argument that dealt in limitless fire and brimstone, and thinned the predestined elect down to a company so small as to be hardly worth the saving. Tom counted the pages of the sermon; after church he always knew how many pages there had been, but he seldom knew anything else about the discourse.

Mark Twain, *The Adventures of Tom Sawyer,* (Penguin Classics), p. 37.

5.2. Defining: Guidance from Scripture

They read from the Book of the Law of God, making it clear and giving the meaning so that the people understood what was being read.

Nehemiah 8:8.

The Teacher searched to find just the right words, and what he wrote was upright and true.

Ecclesiastes 12:10.

This *fourth stage* in the process of preparing a talk is where, preferably with another *digesting* break behind me, I produce the talk that I will preach.

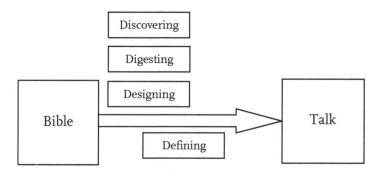

What does this stage involve? It has three aspects: first, I make my final decisions about the shape and contents of the talk; then, I write it out; and finally, I take it for a test drive. This is called the 'defining' stage because I am determining exactly what shape, contents, style, and length my talk will have. Up to this point I have been assembling material and exploring possibilities; now is decision time!

5.3. Checking the Talk

This *first step* means checking all the notes I produced during the previous stages, especially what I wrote down during the *designing* stage and any ideas for change I noted down subsequently.

What I will do at this point depends largely on what I think preaching is all about. If I am governed by the convictions and commitments we surveyed in the first two chapters, I will give first priority to the two basic questions (again!). That is, I will focus again on the *text* and the *context*.

So as I look through my material, the first question I will be asking is, 'Have I been faithful to the *Bible*?' That is, I will be checking to see that I have got the *content* right. This will mean asking the following questions:

- *What?* Is the main point of my talk the main point of the passage?

- *How?* Does the outline of my talk fit the shape of the passage?

- *Why?* Is the application a true expression of the purpose of the passage?

As I check my material, the second question I will be asking is, 'Have I been faithful to my *hearers*?' That is, I will be checking to see that I will make *contact* with them. This will mean asking the following questions:

- Does the talk help them to *receive* the message of the passage?

- Does the talk help them to *respond* to this message?

- Does the talk help them to *remember* the message?

In checking whether my talk is going to make effective contact with the hearers, I will also ask whether it passes the PEST Test. That is, is it Plain, Engaging, Structured, and Targeted?

Once I have satisfied myself that what I have prepared is *as good as I can do in the time that I have,* I take the *second step: I write* the talk. But before we think about what this involves, a quick word about one of the most critical items in a preacher's equipment – the ability to 'live within limits'.

If I had nothing else to do all week except to work on this talk, it could still be improved. 'If only I had just a day or two more!' When this perfectionist anxiety grips me, it's time for a *reality check*. So here's the little clinic I may need to conduct on myself – maybe every week, for the first few months or years!

i. God knows that I have a limited supply of ability and energy (Psalm 103:14).

ii. Yet this week, in addition to preparing this talk, he has also given me other responsibilities, both to him and to other people.

iii. Therefore, God must think it's OK for me to preach a less-than-perfect talk!

Do you see the point? God does *not* expect me to do better than I can do. God does *not* demand of me more than I can give. He will accept 'the best I can do in the circumstances' – and he is also able to use rather mediocre talks to accomplish great things. So when I keep slaving over the talk hour after hour after hour, trying to get it completely right, it is not *God* who is putting this pressure on me! And if I don't quickly work out where the pressure *is* coming from, and take steps to defuse the problem, I am almost certainly going to fall apart sooner or later.

> If God doesn't expect me to do more than I can, the key question we need to ask ourselves is: *Why am I trying to do more than I can?*...At the heart of our busyness is our heart...You need to *identify the desires of your heart that make you try to do more than God expects of you.*[1]

With that out of the way, we now come to what might seem like the easiest part of the process – writing out the talk. *But now is not the time to relax!* Many talks that would have been good have come unstuck within sight of the finishing-line. So what went wrong? Or, to ask the question another way, how can I ensure that I will get this right?

5.4. *Writing the Talk*

There are *three questions* I need to ask myself when I reach this point in the process of preparation. The first issue that I must pay attention to is, 'What am I doing now?' And the answer is, 'I am writing a *talk.*' In other words, I am *not* writing a letter or an essay. The crucial point is that I am writing something people will *hear*, not something they will *read*. How should this control the way I write the talk? The best way of answering that question is to work from the *end* back to the *means*. So, in order to work out what *style* I should use in my talk manuscript, I need to remember what a talk is intended to do and to be. (Think of the

---

[1] Tim Chester, *The Busy Christian's Guide to Busyness*, (Nottingham: IVP, 2006), pp. 78, 80, 84 (his italics).

PEST Test.) When I do that, what writing style will I adopt as a result?

I am writing for the *ear*, not the *eye* – what I am writing is not a piece of writing, but a piece of talking! If I find it difficult to write as I talk, then *I should talk as I write*. What I need to write down is what I would say to people, not what I would write to them.

> The sermon must be written – not as an essay is written, but as a sermon is written; that is to say, with the eyes of a congregation...looking at the writer over his desk.[2]

> Words can make or break your presentation...[You should ask], Are my words clear? Are my words concrete? Are my words simple?[3]

> ...a sermon is not an essay on its hind legs.[4]

In this respect, it is vital that I write the way *I* speak – I should not try to copy someone else's style. If God had wanted me to be like Billy Graham or Barack Obama, he would have made me more like them. I should be myself, speaking as I speak – but speaking as I speak when I want what I am saying to be understood and accepted. So the words I choose will not be rare or fancy but simple and clear, not caviar-and-pâté-de-foie-gras words but meat-and-potatoes words.

> Good hard simple words with good hard clear meanings are good things to use when you speak. They are like pickets in a fence, slim and unimpressive on their own but sturdy and effective when strung together.

> ...don't imitate...high oratory...Say it the way you'd say it if you were speaking, with concentration and respect, to a friend.[5]

If you want a challenge on this front, you might attempt to put these 'ten commandments' into practice when you are writing out your talks!

i.   Always avoid the apt art of alliteration.

ii. Avoid clichés like the plague.

iii. Never, ever generalize.

---

[2]   George A. Buttrick, *Jesus Came Preaching*, (New York: Charles Scribner's Sons, 1932), p. 156f.

[3]   Woodrow M. Kroll, *Prescription for Preaching*, (Grand Rapids: Baker, 1980), p. 58.

[4]   Haddon W. Robinson, *Biblical Preaching*, p. 185.

[5]   Peggy Noonan, *On Speaking Well*, (New York: Regan, 1999), pp. 51, 205.

iv. Do not be redundant or use more words than necessary.

v. One-word sentences? Eliminate!

vi. Don't use contractions.

vii. Exaggeration is a million times worse than understatement.

viii. Foreign words are usually not apropos.

ix. The passive voice is to be avoided.

x. Parenthetical remarks (however relevant) are unnecessary.

The second issue that I must pay attention to is, 'Where will I be when I am giving my talk?' The point is that what I am writing will be *further away* from me *then* than it is *now*. And if I am writing the talk rather than typing it on the computer, I will be looking in a different direction then than I am now – I will be standing straight and looking at the people, rather than leaning forward with my head over the page. How should this control the way I write the talk? Again, thinking about ends will help me to answer this question about means. In order to work out what *format* I should use for my talk manuscript, I need to analyse *why* I have one. What do I need it to do for me while I am preaching? There are three basic requirements my manuscript must meet.

i. I need to be able to *see what is there*. So the words need to be large enough to be read from a distance.

ii. I need to be able to *see where I am up to in the talk*. So my manuscript mustn't look like a page from a book, with continuous text; rather, it needs to be set out with lots of spaces and indenting and the like.

  Because it is important that I can see at a glance where I am and what I should be saying, the manuscript must not be wider than the space my eyes can cover at a glance. You might need to experiment a bit to see what sized sheets of paper are best for you.

iii. The layout of the manuscript should remind me by its appearance, which are the main points, which are the explanations and illustrations, and so on. I might achieve this by using indentation, different colours, different font-sizes, underlining, or all four. Whichever system I use, it needs to make the contents of the page as clear and sharp as possible.

My manuscript might therefore look something like this:

I have a problem with prayer.

It's not that I don't understand prayer sufficiently.

It's that I don't pray enough.

I can explain this problem in various ways.

Sometimes, I justify my lack of prayer by telling myself how little time I have.

But somehow, I manage to have enough time for all the things I really want to do...

really necessary things, like watching the cricket and the football on TV!

Sometimes, I tell myself that praying seems unreal, because it's talking to an invisible presence.

But I have managed perfectly well to cope with other things that seemed unreal

until I got to the point where they seemed normal

things like getting used to wearing spectacles.

Sometimes I explain the problem another way...

But the trouble is I know that these are all just excuses.

I get the distinct impression that you know what I am talking about – that I am speaking for you and not just for me.

So why do we find prayer so difficult?

Why do we find it so hard to be faithful in prayer?

The real issue is very simple – and the Lord Jesus puts his finger right on it in the passage we have just heard.

The third issue I need to consider is what I will preach from: a complete manuscript, or reasonably full notes, or only a brief outline? Whatever I decide about this, it is very helpful – maybe even essential for the first year or two – to *write the talk out in full* at this point in the process. Why? What is the point of doing this if I do not preach from a complete manuscript? The reason is simple: for the sake of my hearers, I want to express the truths of the passage in the most lucid, gripping, and memorable way I can. This will not come without effort! I cannot rely upon the inspiration of the moment, while I am in full flight in the middle of the talk, to supply the words I need.

> Writing is an excellent discipline that helps you in organizing, developing, and forming thoughts into words that communicate clearly and powerfully. You may not read your manuscript to the audience...but writing it out will help you immensely.[6]

What are the pros and cons of the various alternatives?

i. *The complete manuscript.* What is its major advantage? – and what is its most obvious drawback?

> The weakest ink is stronger than the strongest memory. [Chinese proverb]

> ...a lot of writing is essential for most of us. Here are four reasons why: 1. Writing forces clarity... 2. Writing helps to surface fresh thoughts... 3. Writing frees us to go beyond the repetitive phrases we customarily use in conversation... 4. Writing enables us to edit.[7]

> Ferociously frank feedback: 'I have three objections to your sermon: (1) you read it; (2) you didn't read it well; (3) it wasn't worth reading.'

ii. *Speaking without notes.* What is its major advantage? – and what is its most obvious drawback?

> Freedom from notes is worth all that it costs. It depends mainly on three factors in preparation: saturation, organization, and memorization.[8]

> The late Bishop Fulton J Sheen abandoned all notes and

---

[6] Terry G. Carter, J. Scott Duvall, J. Daniel Hays, *Preaching God's Word,* p. 100.

[7] Ken Untener, *Preaching Better,* (New York: Paulist, 1999), p. 48f.

[8] Charles W. Koller, *Expository Preaching Without Notes,* (Grand Rapids: Baker, 1962), p. 85.

written materials...after hearing an elderly Irish lady complain, 'If the father can't remember his own sermon, how can he expect us to remember it?'[9]

iii. *Something in between.* What is its major advantage? – and what is its most obvious drawback?

> ...while I never use a manuscript in preaching, there are five sentences in my sermon which I always write out in advance and know by heart – the first one and the last four.[10]

> Introductions and conclusions should never be read or delivered while depending on copious notes. These two elements of the sermon are critical and need special attention. In the introduction, you are seeking to grab the attention of your audience, so eye contact and natural animation are critical. Dependence on notes can kill the moment. Likewise, in the conclusion you are bringing the heart of the sermon to bear on the audience. Eye contact and animation are just as critical at this phase. You want your first impression (introduction) and your last word (conclusion) to anchor your sermon and highlight your message. Memorization enables you to move away from an overdependence on notes and to connect in a powerful and genuine way with your audience.[11]

> Write out what you mean to say; condense that material into the briefest, barest outline possible; mentally review this summary, again and again, until its content, order, and connecting-links, are easily recalled without reference to notes – until you can 'see your ideas'. Then get up and say what is in mind...[12]

There is no right or wrong here; it is simply a matter of what is the best approach for me to use.

---

[9] David Larsen, *The Anatomy of Preaching,* (Grand Rapids: Baker, 1989), p. 188.
[10] Charles R. Brown, *The Art of Preaching,* (New York: Macmillan, 1922), p. 113.
[11] Terry G. Carter, J. Scott Duvall, J. Daniel Hays, *Preaching God's Word,* p. 164f.
[12] R. E. O. White, *A Guide to Preaching,* p. 150.

5.5.   *Practising the Talk*

This third phase of *defining* my talk is where I make the final decisions about how I will preach it (its *style*) and how much time it will take (its *length* – or should we say 'its *while*'?!).

There are *five* reasons why I should practise the talk after I have written it. The first is that *writing* it is not an adequate preparation for *speaking* it. The only suitable preparation for speaking is – speaking! (It is true, though, that when I am more experienced, I will be reasonably good at writing in the way that I speak. This will make speaking the talk out loud less crucial – but still a *very* good idea!) The more familiar I am with the contents of the talk and with how it sounds, the more likely I am to speak naturally and effectively when I am preaching it.

Secondly, when I have already spoken the talk a couple of times, it is much easier when I am actually preaching it to concentrate on communicating the message to the hearers. Remember our 'learning a musical instrument' analogy? (See page 25.) Just as I want to reach the point where I can concentrate on playing the music rather than playing the instrument, so I want to be able to give all my attention to what I am saying, not to how I am doing.

But when I am inexperienced, and not very confident, what will happen when I am preaching is that all of my attention will be focused on the talk. That is, I will be concentrating on getting it off the page and out of my mouth, hoping not to lose too much on the journey between them! Conversely, my hearers will receive very little attention. However, when I have practised the talk a few times, it is much easier to adjust the focus when I am preaching, so that the hearers – and not the talk, or the preacher – are in the centre of my attention. When I am familiar with what I am going to say, and comfortable with how it sounds when I say it, I can concentrate on saying it *to the people* who are there in front of me.

> Listeners remember the delivery of poor speakers, they remember the content of good speakers...Excellent delivery disappears from the awareness of the listener. Thus, the goal of the preacher is to get out of the way of the message...We achieve this goal by practising sound delivery skills until they become so natural to us that we use them as unconsciously as we would in

conversation...Let no one make you ashamed of practising. Great communicators are made, not born...Practice in the early stages of ministry is especially crucial.[13]

Effective delivery is largely dependent upon practice. It takes practice to be natural before an audience.[14]

Don't prepare in silence for that which is meant to be spoken aloud. By this I mean don't just think the sermon through or review the script in silence. Speak it out loud and standing up...[15]

The third reason for 'preaching' the talk before I preach it is so that I can iron out the wrinkles. It is often not until I hear the words that I realize which of them are problematic in one way or another. Some might be difficult to say without stumbling; others might easily be confused with similar-sounding words

Once you've finished a first draft...stand up and read it aloud. *Where you falter, alter.* Sentences must be short and sayable not only for you but for your listeners.

*...give your speech before you give it...*This is where you'll discover such problems as unpronounceable words, undeliverable sentences, and unpersuasive arguments.[16]

The fourth reason for practising the talk is that this will prevent it from taking too long. Experienced preachers generally have a clear idea of how long it takes them to preach a page of their manuscript, but if I am a beginner I am unlikely to know the answer to this vital question. So when I practice my talk, I might get a surprise! It might be much shorter than I expected. If that is the case, I needn't worry about it – I will just preach what I've got, knowing that it will bring some benefit to the hearers. (Remember Isaiah 55:10-11.) In any case, I haven't really got time to make major changes to the talk at this point.

On the other hand, I might find that the talk is much longer than I expected. If so, I probably do need to do something about it. I need to be merciful to my hearers – I need to get the pruning shears out

---

[13]   Bryan Chapell, *Christ-Centered Preaching*, p. 331, with footnote 3.
[14]   Woodrow M. Kroll, *Prescription for Preaching*, p. 130.
[15]   Thomas R. Swears, *Preaching to Head and Heart*, p. 131.
[16]   Peggy Noonan, *On Speaking Well*, pp. 35, 206 (her italics).

and do some lopping! It is better that they hear the first half of a good talk that they will remember, than all of a talk that lasted so long that they will forget the whole lot. As the wise Teacher recognized long ago: 'The more the words, the less the meaning, and how does that profit anyone?' (Ecclesiastes 6:11)

The fifth reason for practising the talk is that I can then preach from notes or summaries, instead of a full manuscript. Unless I am very familiar with the contents, the sequence, and the phraseology of the talk, I am unlikely to preach effectively with anything less than a complete manuscript – simply because I may be too nervous about having a memory lapse at a critical moment. If (as I should) I take a lot of trouble to find the most memorable and powerful ways of expressing the contents of the talk when I write it, it is a great pity to forget the vital words just before I am about to say them!

Finally, a word of warning: I am bound to feel stupid when I practise my talk out loud by myself! So it is a good idea to find a location where I am so unlikely to be seen or overheard that I can let it rip without fear of being caught. In the garden shed; in some nearby bushland; in the back lane behind a saw-mill – the world is full of possibilities!

5.6. How Long, O Lord?

Does preparing a talk really have to be this complex and time-consuming? Won't it be possible to take shortcuts? If so, isn't it OK to take them? The answer depends on what the question is getting at. If it means, 'Is it obligatory to follow the process of preparation set out in this book?' the answer is, 'no.' If it means, 'Does preparing a Bible talk take a lot of time and require a lot of effort?' the answer is, almost always, 'yes.' If it means, 'Can I use a method that takes much less time and effort?' the answer is, 'why?' What motivation lies behind this version of the question? Does it reflect an honourable desire to use my time wisely as God's servant – or a self-centred desire to take the easy way out?

Because there are no direct commandments about this in Scripture, we are free to approach the matter of preparing a talk in any way that proves suitable (1 Corinthians 10:23). So the questions we need to think through are these:

- What kinds of shortcut could I take?

- What is likely to happen if I take them?

- In what circumstances would it be OK to take them?

5.7.   *Help!*

This all sounds very daunting! Is it realistic to think that I can master all of this and become a good preacher? Or is this really beyond the likes of me? The answer is that I can indeed learn to prepare and preach a Bible talk that will benefit the hearers. The keys are simple:

i.   I need to understand the principles well.

ii.   I need to practise the skills often.

iii. I need to learn from good models. (Actually, even bad models will do – as long as I can work out where they went wrong, so that I don't repeat their mistakes.)

GOT IT?

i.   What tests should I use when assessing the suitability of possible outlines for a talk?

ii.   How is writing a talk different from other kinds of writing?

iii. What does the layout of the written talk need to do for me?

iv.   Why do I need to practise a talk before I give it?

6.   Delivering

6.1.   Delivering: To get you thinking...

...the religious life of Shepperton was falling back towards low-water mark. Here, you perceive, was a terrible stronghold of Satan; and you may well pity the Rev. Amos Barton, who had to stand single-handed and summon it to surrender. We read, indeed, that the walls of Jericho fell down before the sound of trumpets; but we nowhere hear that those trumpets were hoarse and feeble. Doubtless they were trumpets that gave forth clear and ringing tones, and sent a mighty vibration through brick and mortar. But the oratory of the Rev. Amos resembled rather a Belgian railway-horn, which shows praiseworthy intentions inadequately fulfilled.

George Eliot, 'The Sad Fortunes of the Reverend Amos Barton' in *Scenes of Clerical Life*, p. 19.

Mr Hooper had the reputation of a good preacher, but not an energetic one: he strove to win his people heavenward, by mild persuasive influences, rather than to drive them thither, by the thunders of the Word.

Nathaniel Hawthorne, 'The Minister's Black Veil: A Parable' in William C. Spengemann [ed.], *The Portable Hawthorne*, p. 68.

...Pastor Ingqvist's faithful critic...says of the pastor's sermons, 'He mumbles. He murmurs. It's a lot of on-the-one-hand-this, on-the-other-hand-that. He never comes straight out. He never puts the hay down where the goats can get it. It's a lot of talk, and many a Sunday I've walked away with no idea *what* he said. Can't remember even where he started from. You never had that problem with the old preachers. There was never a moment's doubt. It was Repent or Be Damned. We need that. This guy, he tries to please everybody. Just once I wish he'd raise his voice and pound on the pulpit. That way I'd know he wasn't talking in his sleep.'

Garrison Keilor, *Lake Wobegon Days*, (London: Faber & Faber, 1986), pp. 376-7.

The *Black-Vested Road Runner* is also known as the *Pacing Puffin*. This type of pulpit bird is known for a certain restlessness that is a distinct characteristic of this species. His church birds are recognized for having the largest number of sore necks per capita of any flock in the aviary. The *Road Runner* simply cannot stay on his perch for the duration of his sermon. For minor points of emphasis, he normally flits from one side of the pulpit to the other. But when describing the travails of Old Testament heroes, he generally swoops up and down the entire length of the platform.

LeRoy Koopman, *Guide to Ecclesiastical Birdwatching*, p. 44.

When I hear a man preach, I like to see him act as if he were fighting bees.

Abraham Lincoln, quoted in Nicolas Bentley [ed.], *The Treasury of Humorous Quotations*, (London: J. M. Dent, 1962), p. 127.

You say in your letter that you went and heard the philosopher when his ship put in where you are. 'His words,' you say, 'tend to be tumbled out at a tremendous pace, pounded and driven along...' You should take the view...that this copious and impetuous energy in a speaker is better suited to a hawker than to someone who deals with a subject of serious importance... Language...which devotes its attention to truth should be plain and unadorned. This popular style has nothing to do with truth. Its object is to sway a mass audience, to carry away unpractised ears by the force of its onslaught.

Seneca, *Letters from a Stoic*, (Penguin Classics), (London: Penguin, 2004 [65 AD]), p. 82-83.

Then the preacher began to preach; and begun in earnest, too; and went weaving first to one side of the platform and then the other, and a leaning down over the front of it, with his arms and his body going all the time, and shouting his words out with all his might; and every now and then he would hold up his Bible and spread it open, and kind of pass it around this way and that...

Mark Twain, *Adventures of Huckleberry Finn*, edited with an Introduction and Notes by Henry Nash Smith, (Cambridge, Mass: The Riverside Press, 1958 [1884]), p. 111.

6.2. *Delivering: Guidance from Scripture*

After they had prayed, the place where they were meeting was shaken. And they were all filled with the Holy Spirit and spoke the word of God boldly.

Acts 4:31.

Some preachers are so outstanding that each of their talks is followed by a great awakening! We won't be aiming to copy them now that we have come to the business end of the process: *delivering* the talk. This is where we get to preach the Bible talk we have worked so hard to prepare.

In the previous sessions we have seen all kinds of ways in which my understanding of what preaching is will shape what I prepare and how I prepare it. The same goes for preaching it! How I deal with the issues involved depends mostly upon what convictions I have about preaching. As always, 'know-what' and 'know-why' are more fundamental than 'know-how'. So what are the challenges I will face in preaching my Bible talk?

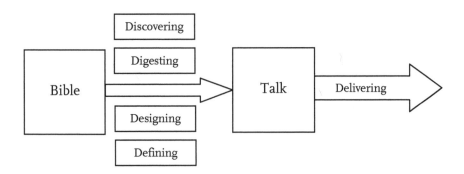

What does 'delivering' a talk mean? Much the same as 'delivering' a letter. If I write to you, my letter is delivered, not when I drop it into the mailbox but when the postman brings it to your home. It has to be transported from where I am to where you are. In the same way, a talk is delivered when it arrives: that is, when it is *heard,* not just when it is *spoken.* So how can I ensure that my talk is 'delivered'? How do I speak so that my talk makes real and effective contact with the hearers? The answer involves both my outside and my inside.

A spoken message is made up of only three components: the *verbal,* the *vocal,* and the *visual...* The verbal element is the message itself – the words you say. Most of us tend to concentrate only on the verbal element, mistakenly assuming this to be the message, when in fact it is only *part* of the message. The second part of the message is the vocal element – the intonation, projection, and resonance of your voice as it carries the words. And the third part is the visual element – what people see – the motion and expression of your body and face as you speak...When we learn how to coordinate all three of these components to form one totally consistent message...*we have impact.*[1]

6.3.   *The Outside of the Preacher*

There are two issues to be considered here: my equipment and my manner. The first requirement for effective delivery is that my 'equipment' – what I use to get the message across to the hearers –is in good working order. I have *two* instruments at my disposal, and I must ensure that both of them function as well as possible.

> The preacher uses brain and muscle. This means that he should train for his task with the same devotion that the [sportsman] applies to his. This means sleep. Too many parishes listen to preachers spent and fatigued with last-minute preparation and a short night's rest. The steward of God's mysteries is also a steward of the body which is his tool.[2]

> When you preach, your audience has no perception of titles, paragraphs, italics or bold print...or any such features of visual design. All they have to go on is the sounds you make and the body movements you associate with them...Everything you communicate must be done with those words and any physical movements, gestures, or facial expressions you use to enhance them.[3]

---

[1]   Hershael W. York & Bert Decker, *Preaching with BOLD Assurance,* pp. 201, 203.
[2]   Richard R. Caemmerer, *Preaching for the Church,* (St Louis: Concordia, 1959), p. 123.
[3]   Wayne McDill, *12 Essential Skills for Great Preaching,* 2nd ed., (Nashville: Broadman & Holman, 2006), p. 202.

The first of these instruments is *my voice*. Unless I stand up and speak, a talk won't be preached – and unless I speak up when I stand up, a talk won't be delivered! Because a talk is not delivered unless it is heard, when I preach I must speak up, speak out, and speak well.

I must speak *up:* the volume must be loud enough for the people seated furthest away to hear me. The best way of ensuring that this happens is to speak to those people! Unfortunately, when I am feeling nervous and lack confidence, I will tend to speak too softly (and often too quickly as well). As a result, the people who are not close to me may well find it difficult to catch what I am saying. So in my preaching I need – consciously and deliberately – to speak up, aiming to be heard by the people farthest from me.

I must also speak *out:* that is, I must project my voice to the back row.

You can put your mind into your sermon, and you can put your heart into it; but until you put your diaphragm into it, it won't amount to much.[4]

Here again nerves can interfere, as nervous preachers often look down at their notes much of the time. When I am not looking up, I am not speaking out; my voice is directed downwards to my notes, not outwards to those who are trying to hear me. So even if my voice is loud enough, the people some distance from me might still not be able to hear me clearly. Projecting my voice is as important as raising my voice – and this will only happen if I choose, consciously and deliberately, to look up, not down. Making this important choice is the most effective way of dealing with something else that hinders talk delivery. If I am speaking up and out it will be more difficult for me to speak too quickly. When I am looking at people, the unconscious feedback cues that shape our face-to-face communication will be at work. Largely automatically, I will adjust the pace of my delivery to suit the hearers.

But do I really have to be concerned about this? After all, in most places where I am likely to preach there will be a microphone and sound system to project my voice. True, but that doesn't change the fact that I need to speak up and speak out. The sound system will take care of the volume, to ensure that my voice is loud enough to be heard by those

---

4   Quoted in Ilion T. Jones, *Principles and Practice of Preaching,* (New York: Abingdon, 1956), p. 207.

farthest from me. But it is still me, and not the microphone, who needs to speak to them. While they cannot be engaged by a talk they cannot hear, the hearers are most likely to be engaged by – to feel involved, to have a sense of participation with – a preacher who speaks to them.

Because the voice is the indispensable instrument of our preaching, it is vital that we understand not only how to use it but also how to care for it and, where necessary, to improve it. Preachers should be no less committed than actors and singers to ways of developing and protecting the voice.

> As the hammer is to the carpenter, the scalpel to the surgeon, the trowel to the brick mason or the needle to the tailor, so the voice is to the preacher...yet how often we who are called to impart the most important truths in the world are apt to neglect, if not wilfully abuse, our all-vital 'tool of the trade'!

> ...large numbers of preachers experience voice problems out of failure to observe even the most basic rules of voice care. Singers, actors and schoolteachers seem to be more conscientious in this area than heralds of the gospel. This should never be so.[5]

This applies especially to the voice as that which conveys meaning to the hearers. For this to occur, I must speak *well*. In the first place, this means that I need to articulate clearly: 'Unless you speak intelligible words with your tongue, how will anyone know what you are saying? You will just be speaking into the air.' (1 Corinthians 14:9).

> Three women were discussing what they had heard their friend say to her husband. The first said she was talking about animals, because she had mentioned 'trained deer'. The second said that she was asking him to find out about 'the train, dear'. The third said they were discussing music, because the woman had referred to a 'trained ear'. When they asked her which of them had heard correctly, the woman replied that none of them had: because she had been away, she was asking her husband whether it 'had rained here'!

---

5   Mike Mellor, *Look After Your Voice: Taking Care of the Preacher's Greatest Asset,* (Leominster: Day One, 2008), pp. 9, 13.

If my nerves cause me to speak too softly or too quickly, my hearers are likely to miss some of what I am saying – so I will need to take steps to ensure that I do not slur or jumble my words, but pronounce them distinctly and clearly. Speaking well also means using the right tone of voice for each point I am making – whether asserting or questioning, being humorous or serious, issuing an appeal or a warning, expressing sympathy or surprise. The extent to which I can do this will reflect how carefully and how often I have practised my talk before I deliver it. When I have been through it several times, I will be much better able to concentrate on the meanings rather than the words, and my tone of voice will tend to look after itself.

The second instrument at my disposal is *my body*. Is it really necessary to say anything about this? Surely all I need to worry about is that people can hear me? Let me respond to your question with one of my own: in these hi-tech days, why don't I record my talk on a DVD and have that played during the meeting? In fact, this would enable me to preach at any number of places at the same time – and think how much faster and wider the Word of God could spread if all preachers did this! So why don't we do it this way? For probably the same reason that God did not give us his Word by lowering a megaphone through the clouds and making periodic broadcasts. Instead, he sent human messengers to speak his Word – and finally he sent his Son, both to bring and to be his Word to the world. In preaching, God's Word comes to us not through a disembodied voice but through a person who speaks to us.

So, yes, this is an important dimension of delivering my talk. The people who are *hearing* what I am preaching are also *seeing* me while I preach it. Effective communication is a result of what they see as well as what they hear. If I want my talk to have maximum impact, I will need to ensure that, in addition to my voice, my eyes, my face, and my hands all play their part.

i.   My *eyes* must be involved: I must look at my hearers. It is very difficult to have a conversation with someone who doesn't ever look at me. In the same way, it is very difficult for people to have a sense of participation in my preaching if I never look at them. I do not need to look directly at every individual, but I do need to look towards the hearers. The larger the group is to which I am speaking, the more deliberate my looking at them needs to be. When I have only twenty or thirty people in front of me, unless they are very spread out I can easily see them all by looking straight ahead. But when I am speaking to a hundred or more, I need to ensure that I look to my left and to my right as well as straight ahead of me. If I do not do so, lots of my hearers will feel left out because I am always looking somewhere else.

ii. My *face* should also be involved. When I have a conversation with someone, my facial expressions support the message being conveyed by my words. This is, in fact, a quite important aspect of interpersonal communication. But this is not something I have to think about consciously: my facial expressions occur automatically as I talk – because I am focused on what I want to get across. The same will be true in my preaching. If I am concentrating on communicating the message to my hearers, my face will do its part by becoming animated in the right ways at the right time.

iii. It is good for my *hands* to be involved as well. Again, when I am talking to someone, my hands are usually playing their part in the communication process. This will differ from person to person, of course. Some of us don't normally make many hand gestures, while others would find it almost impossible to talk at all if our hands were tied behind our back! While there is no need for preaching to include dramatic gestures, I must at least give my hands an opportunity to play their part. They will not be able to do so if they are gripping the sides of the lectern or trapped in my trouser pockets. But if I stand up straight and leave my hands free, they will know when and how to make their contribution. I can safely leave them to do that without needing to rehearse any gestures in advance. (It is far better to have only one or two during the talk that are obviously natural, than any number that are obviously unnatural.)

The *second* requirement for effective delivery of my talk is my *manner*. This means the way I approach the hearers, how I 'come across'. What manner should I have when I preach? As should be obvious by now, I can only answer this question rightly by remembering what preaching is all about. In fact, if I know what I should be doing in my preaching, and if I concentrate on doing it, then my manner will largely take care of itself. That is why we dealt with this issue in Chapter 1, when we analysed what will characterize our preaching when we are communicating God's Word. We saw then that such preaching will combine earnestness and calmness; it will be done with conviction and also with confidence in God. It will also combine authority and humility, because I am communicating a message that is from God and also for me, as well as for my hearers. Now we need to add one more characteristic – in my preaching I need to be myself; I need to speak *naturally*.

> If humility is the proper attitude for the speaker with reference to God and God's Word, then genuineness...is the proper attitude of the speaker with reference to the congregation.[6]

6.4. *The Inside of the Preacher*

There is another issue I face as a preacher. I don't want people just to hear me speaking; I want them to hear me speaking *to* them. And I want to speak to them so that I reach them – I want to communicate effectively. Why? Because I want my Bible talk to convey God's message to them. And there lies my greatest problem as a novice preacher: I am likely to be very nervous – and that is bound to get in the way of effective communication. But even the experienced preacher will find that this remains an issue. So how can I ensure that nerves don't get the better of me?

The problem nerves pose for the preacher is that they give me the double-whammy: they get me before I start preaching – and they get me again after I have finished! We need to take a quick look at both of these, so that we can soften their impact – and maybe even benefit from what happens.

First, it is highly likely that I will get nervous *before I preach*. This is not by itself a bad thing, for what is happening is that my adrenalin system is firing up. This is my 'fight or flight' mechanism – the way God has equipped us to handle challenges and face dangers. So my nerves – perspiring; getting 'butterflies in the stomach'; trembling; feeling light-headed and so on – are, in part, a result of the fact that I believe that preaching matters. One of the reasons I am nervous is that I want my talk to do good to the hearers. If I didn't care about what happened, I wouldn't be nervous. (There might well be other less worthy reasons for my nerves, of course. I might be nervous because I don't want to be a 'failure', and so on. Even preachers are infected by sin!)

---

[6]   Dietrich Bonhoeffer, *Worldly Preaching: Lectures on Homiletics*, (New York: Crossroad, 1991 [1935-39]), p. 142.

Tension cannot be avoided, need not be feared, but must be understood. Tension is bodily preparation, the way God has made us to enable us to meet emergencies and difficult situations. Tension makes us alert...So long as tension is the speaker's servant, tension is good.[7]

Nervousness keys us up; fright paralyzes: nervousness ensures our best; fright ensures our worst: nervousness comes of a realization that God has given us a great task; fright comes of a suspicion that we are not equal to it.[8]

It is important that a man should approach the moment of preaching with a mind looking outward to others, and to God, and not inward to his own misgivings, unworthiness, or 'nerves'. He *is* doing God's work...in all our scattering of the seeds of truth, the Sower Himself is still at work.[9]

So nervousness itself is not a bad thing; however, the unconscious effects it has on me may be quite a different story! Facial tics, weird body postures, unnatural voice quality – these and many other distractions have been inflicted on congregations by nervous preachers. If these things happen to me, I need kind friends who will tell me, so that I can work on eliminating them (the habits, not the friends!).

With nerves, the *most crucial moments* are the first few seconds before I launch into the talk. Once I have quickly put my Bible and my manuscript in place, I need quite deliberately to look at the people in front of me for a few seconds, and then to begin speaking while I am still looking at the hearers. Why is this? Because this will determine whether my nerves control my talk or my talk controls my nerves! I know what I am about to say, because I have learned the opening sentence(s) by heart. Therefore I don't need to focus all my attention on choosing my words or on checking my notes. As a result, I can give all of my attention to the hearers. If I do so for a few seconds before I begin speaking, two things are highly likely to happen: (a) they will have become attentive, and (b) I will have become less nervous. However, when I am nervous, any silence seems to last forever – so it is a good

---

[7]   Jay E. Adams, *Pulpit Speech*, p. 156.
[8]   P. E. Sangster, *Speech in the Pulpit*, (London: Epworth, 1958), p. 4.
[9]   R. E. O. White, *A Guide to Preaching*, p. 152f.

idea to count off the seconds in my head. ('One humpty, two humpty, three humpty, four' is just about the right length if I say it steadily. It's a good idea to make sure I don't move my lips while I am doing this, though – especially if any experienced lip-readers are present!)

The *second* problem I face with 'nerves' is what happens *after I preach*. We will take a look at this in the next chapter.

Perhaps you have noticed the glaring omission from this chapter. Our discussion about what to do and how to do it has made no reference to our prayerful dependence upon God – but could there be anything worse than speaking about God for God without God?! It is vital that every aspect of our preaching is bathed in prayer, from when I begin my preparation until after I have given my talk.

> ...by praying for himself and for those he is about to address, [the preacher] must become a man of prayer before becoming a man of words.[10]

GOT IT?

i.   How should I use my voice in preaching?

ii. What 'preaching equipment' do I have apart from my voice? How should I use it?

iii. What is the best way of dealing with my nervousness before I begin speaking?

---

[10]   Augustine, *On Christian Teaching*, p. 121.

PART 3

PROGRESS

Progress: To get you thinking...

Improving your sermon delivery is a process of learning, failing, relearning, practicing, and then practicing some more. Don't expect miracles, but devote yourself to improving little by little over time.

Terry G. Carter, J. Scott Duvall, J. Daniel Hays, *Preaching God's Word*, p. 167.

Up to and including his last sermon, the preacher remains a learner.

Brian A. Greet in John Stacey [ed.], *In Church*, 2nd ed. (London: Methodist Church, 1975), p. 132.

...there ought to be a constant exposure to good models... Where are the good models to whom we should draw near and from whom we should learn?...first of all, the biblical preachers themselves. We ought to read the prophets and the apostles and our Lord, not only to know what they said...but also to know how they spoke.

A. N. Martin, *Prepared to Preach*, 2nd ed., (Strathpine North: Covenanter, 1986), pp. 33-4.

Lengthening experience can either deepen insight and develop maturer skills, or it can harden habit and perpetuate mistakes. It cannot be said too plainly, or too often, that in preaching a man has never done learning, nor does he ever get beyond the need for watchfulness... in time he comes to think either that he knows it all, or that he is too experienced to change.

R. E. O. White, *A Guide to Preaching*, p. 157.

Don't be discouraged if your progress in preaching seems to be slow. Just make sure you are going in the right direction...There is always something new to learn in the vast field of communicating the Word to modern man.

Warren W. and David W. Wiersbe, *Making Sense of the Ministry*, 2nd ed., (Grand Rapids: Baker, 1989), p. 112.

The better you are, the less people notice you. The greater your ability to present God's Word, the less you get in the way and the freer your listeners are to hear the message and to respond personally. And *that* is why we take the time to learn how to communicate better.

Hershael W York & Bert Decker, *Preaching with BOLD Assurance*, p. 224.

Introductory thoughts

This section of the book is based on one fundamental conviction – that anyone who has the ability to serve God as a preacher also has the ability to become increasingly effective in this ministry.

This kind of growth will not come without hard work, carried out in dependence upon God – but it will happen, if we go about it the right way. What is the 'right way'? Essentially, it means continuing to work hard at preparing and delivering the best talks we can give. It also includes such things as learning from good books about preaching, learning from preachers who are good models, and getting supportive and constructive feedback about our talks, alerting us to good things that can be strengthened and weaknesses that need attention. All of this needs to be done with the aim of becoming a better preacher, and with the conviction that this is possible.

7.   Debriefing

7.1.   *Debriefing: To get you thinking...*

After the sermon...we stand in danger of several things. Affected by the uneasiness that seems inherent to the period following the sermon we are impelled to seek a conversation that will minister to us...we nervously question others as to their opinion of how things went. A favorable judgment will satisfy our vanity. But our actual uneasiness remains unsatisfied and is only covered over...The preacher's lack of peace after the sermon is also rooted in the temptation toward unbelief.

Dietrich Bonhoeffer, *Worldly Preaching*, p. 145f.

Later on in the evening...the Rev. Amos Barton drew from his pocket a thin green-covered pamphlet, and, presenting it to the Countess, said, –

'You were pleased, I think, with my sermon on Christmas Day. It has been printed in *The Pulpit*, and I thought you might like a copy.'

'That indeed I shall. I shall quite value the opportunity of reading that sermon. There was such depth in it! – such argument! It was not a sermon to be heard only once...'

The sermon in question...was an extremely argumentative one on the Incarnation; which, as it was preached to a congregation not one of whom had any doubt of that doctrine, and to whom the Socinians therein confuted were as unknown as the Arimaspians, was exceedingly well adapted to trouble and confuse the Sheppertonian mind.

George Eliot, 'The Sad Fortunes of the Reverend Amos Barton' in *Scenes of Clerical Life*, p. 30.

[They] entered, all with that brisk and cheerful air which a sermon is often observed to produce when it is quite finished.

George Eliot, 'Mr Gilfil's Love-Story' in *Scenes of Clerical Life*, p. 134.

The eloquent voice, on which the souls of the listening audience had been borne aloft, as on the swelling waves of the sea, at length came to a pause. There was a momentary silence, profound as what should follow the utterance of oracles. Then ensued a murmur and half-hushed tumult; as if the auditors, released from the high spell that had transported them...were returning into themselves, with all their awe and wonder still heavy on them. In a moment more, the crowd began to gush forth from the doors of the church...How fared it with him then?...How feeble and pale he looked amid all his triumph! The energy – or say, rather, the inspiration which had held him up, until he should have delivered the sacred message that brought its own strength along with it from heaven – was withdrawn, now that it had so faithfully performed its office. The glow, which they had just before beheld burning on his cheek, was extinguished, like a flame that sinks down hopelessly among the late-decaying embers. It seemed hardly the face of a man alive, with such a deathlike hue; it was hardly a man with life in him...

Nathaniel Hawthorne, 'The Scarlet Letter' in William C. Spengemann [ed.], *The Portable Hawthorne*, p. 343f.

Our sufficiency is of God: our efficiency is largely of our own making, the reward of intelligent dedication, and given to workmen who, though they dare not become conceited, take care that they need not be ashamed.

R. E. O. White, *A Guide to Preaching*, p. 4.

7.2.   Debriefing: Guidance from Scripture

You know, brothers and sisters, that our visit to you was not without results... but with the help of God we dared to tell you his gospel ... the appeal we make does not spring from error or impure motives, nor are we trying to trick you... We are not trying to please people but God, who tests our hearts. You know we never used flattery, nor did we put on a mask to cover up greed—God is our witness.

1 Thessalonians 2:1-5.

This is the final stage in the process that began when I read and prayed over my passage. As far as this book is concerned, that was back in

Chapter 3. Now that I have given my talk, the time has come to assess both the talk itself and also my delivery of it. But *when* and *how* should this be done?

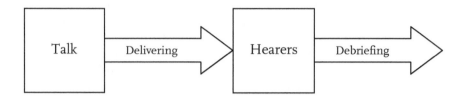

7.3.   *Evaluating Preaching*

Like many other aspects of preaching, there will be different ways of approaching this issue amongst preachers. However, the basic matters are fairly self-evident:

i.   I *must* evaluate my preaching – because I want to become steadily more effective as a preacher of God's Word.

ii.   I *must not* try to evaluate a talk too soon after preaching it – because my adrenalin-related let-down will mean that I am in no condition to see things objectively. If I have preached in the morning, then I might be ready to engage in worthwhile assessment that evening; if I have preached in the evening, I should leave evaluation until sometime the next day.

> ...following the emotion, exhilaration, excitement or despondency of delivering our sermon, we should avoid the temptation for immediate self-evaluation of our own preaching.[1]

iii.   I *must not* try to evaluate my preaching on my own – because the most important areas where problems are occurring and change is needed are the very things I am least likely to be aware of. Who can I get to help me? It does not need to be a preacher, but the person(s) I ask for help need to be (a) aware of what to look for in a Bible talk and its preacher, (b) confident enough to give me honest feedback, and (c) kind enough to do it in a

---

[1]   Derek Newton, *And the Word Became...A Sermon*, (Fearn: Christian Focus, 2003), p. 245.

constructive and encouraging way – and not like this ferociously frank feedback!:

> That sermon was like a glass of water thrown to a drowning man.

> Each of your sermons is better than the one that follows it.

As I learn by experience how to assess my talks objectively, I will find that I can bring a different perspective that complements what my friendly critics have to say. Often this will concern those things about a talk that only become clear by giving it. Although weaknesses will sometimes become evident when I practise the talk, it is often only when I deliver the talk to a group of people that I can pick up the ways in which it needs to be corrected and improved.

What should I and my helpers be evaluating? What we want to assess is how far my preaching achieved its goals. What is the best way of doing this? The simplest and most straightforward way is to use the same checklist that I used in my preparation – that is, we will measure my preaching by using the *content* and *contact* questions. So as we review the talk, the first question we will ask is, 'Was I faithful to the *Bible?*' This will mean asking the following questions:

- *What?* Was the main point of my talk the main point of the passage?

- *How?* Did the outline of my talk fit the shape of the passage?

- *Why?* Was the application a true expression of the purpose of the passage?

The second question we will ask is, 'Was I faithful to my *hearers?*' This will mean asking the following questions:

- Did the talk help them to *receive* the message of the passage? That is, did it do a good job of the Explanation task?

- Did the talk help them to *respond* to this message? That is, did it do a good job of the Application task?

- Did the talk help them to *remember* the message? That is, did it do a good job of the Formulation task – was it well structured and well worded?

In assessing how well I did these things, it will also be helpful to use the 'PEST Test', by considering the extent to which my talk was Plain,

Engaging, Structured, and Targeted. Finally, we will want to assess how well I delivered the talk – that is, did I use my voice and face and hands effectively to get the message across?

This kind of evaluation will put me in a position to answer two important questions about the future.

7.4. Does this Talk have a Future?

The answer is, 'It all depends!' On what? In the first place, on who you ask, for preachers have different views about this matter. As the following quotations show, some do not believe in re-using talks while others regard this as a very profitable thing to do.

> I keep old sermons, not to preach them again, but rather to make sure that I don't preach them again!...when God wanted to teach his people that 'man does not live by bread alone but on every word that comes from the mouth of the Lord,' he did it by sending manna. But the Israelites could only gather enough manna for that day itself; it couldn't be stored and reused. I believe that our sermons, too, should be fresh each day. Unlike vintage port, they don't improve with keeping![2]

> ...you will find that sermons grow and develop as the result of being preached. You do not see everything when you are preparing in your study; you will see further aspects while you are preaching...[So, when it is repeated, though the preacher is] basically preaching the same sermon, in many senses it is not the same sermon; it becomes a better sermon...[In addition] as you become familiar with your sermon it will greatly add to the effectiveness of your preaching of that sermon. There is less sense of strain, and you are not concentrating to the same extent on trying to remember what you have to say. You have attained to a measure of freedom because you are now familiar with the material in a way that you could not be when you preached it for the first time.[3]

I think the second of these approaches makes better sense than the first.

---

[2]   Simon Coupland, *Stripping Preaching to its Bare Essentials*, pp. 27-8.

[3]   Martyn Lloyd-Jones, *Preaching and Preachers*, pp. 286-7.

In fact, I think we should ask, 'If a talk is not worth repeating, was it worth preaching the first time?' To which the right answer is, 'It all depends!' On what this time? I think it is appropriate to repeat a talk when the following things are true:

i.   It has survived the evaluation process – that is, when my friendly critics saw no need to make drastic changes to it, and gave it a generally favourable response.

ii. The reason for preaching it initially was not determined by a very specific need in one particular place – that is, when it is general enough to be heard by other people than those who heard it the first time.

iii. I want to preach it again, because it says something important – that is, when my reason for reusing it is not that I can't be bothered preparing a new one!

What do you think about this? Can you see yourself giving the same talk more than once?

7.5.   Does this Preacher have a Future?

When what fired it up is all over, my adrenalin system switches off – and I usually crash with it! For preachers, this is often 'the birth of the blues'. The particular impact this has on me depends to a large extent on my temperament. However, a pattern that is quite common goes like this: in the hour or two after preaching, I am on a 'high' – but then I descend quite quickly into a hole that is as far below normality as my 'high' was above it. And when I have hit the bottom, I not only feel wrung out, but I also struggle with doubts and with feelings of inadequacy or failure.

The more of myself I have invested in the talk, the further down I am likely to plunge. Typical reactions (with increasing degrees of bleakness) are:

- 'That was a hopeless talk.'
- 'I'm a hopeless preacher.'
- 'Preaching is a pointless exercise.'

Once I realize what is happening – that my 'fight and flight' systems are protesting because they have taken a bit of a hammering – I will also realize that I don't need to take these reactions too seriously. This then frees me up in two ways.

First, I can cease treating my bleak thoughts as symptoms of a profound spiritual crisis. It took me ages to learn this – so let me share my story with you just in case you are inclined to be as much of a slow-learner as I am. When I was a pastor, I used to have these grey sessions quite regularly on Mondays. It never occurred to me that I was misinterpreting what was happening until I came across a fellow-minister during one summer holiday. He was sitting under a tree reading a book about stress and burnout amongst pastors. It was called, *Never Resign On A Monday*. As soon as I saw the title, the penny dropped! What I had foolishly regarded as signs of spiritual failure were just the natural results of let down after a busy Sunday in which I would normally give one talk twice in the morning and a different one in the evening.

Secondly, I can put my negative feelings in their place by ignoring them while I do something enjoyable and refreshing – while saying the last bit of 1 Timothy 6:17 frequently to myself! In other words, I can train myself to live *with* these feelings rather than *in* them. In this regard, we can all benefit from the wise advice implied by the following snapshot of a pastor's Sunday.

> [Having] preached in the morning...[at] night he thinks it a very fit time, both sutable to the joy of the day, and without hinderance to publick duties, either to entertaine some of his neighbours, or to be entertained of them...As he opened the day with prayer, so he closeth it, humbly beseeching the Almighty to pardon and accept our poor services, and to improve them, that we may grow therein, and that our feet may be like hindes feet ever climbing up higher, and higher unto him.[4]

I hope I haven't given you the impression that there is no spiritual dimension to this struggle, as there most certainly is. Yet this spiritual dimension is the *fruit* of my dark thoughts and negative feelings and not their *root*, for they have a natural cause. This spiritual dimension has two sides to it – one concerns the way both my own sinfulness and the

---

[4] George Herbert, *The Country Parson and Selected Poems*, (A Treasury of Christian Books), (London: SCM, 1956 [1652]), p. 27.

Enemy use these thoughts and feelings, and the other has to do with whether and how I relate them to God.

As to the first of these: there are any number of ways in which the Enemy can team up with my own sinful tendencies to extract as much harm as possible from the 'post-preaching blues'. Which ones are most likely for me will depend on my personality type. It might be as simple as having me wallow in self pity; it might involve dark doubts about the rightness of me being a preacher; it might even extend to blaming God for putting me through such trials. It is very important that I know myself well enough to recognize where I am most vulnerable; it is also important that I am realistic about the opposition of the Enemy – after all, as the apostle Paul reminds us, 'we are not unaware of his schemes' (2 Corinthians 2:11).

He who knows neither self nor enemy will fail in every battle.[5]

The spiritual dimension of this issue also concerns how I relate to God in and about the 'blues'. In the end, the choice we face is very simple – we can either struggle with it on our own, or we can take it to God, confident that we will 'receive mercy and find grace to help us in our time of need' (Hebrews 4:16). In view of what awaits us at 'the throne of grace', it makes no sense at all to take the first of these options.

7.6.   And finally ...

As you have progressed through this book, you may have found yourself moving from disbelief to discouragement to dismay to despair. At first, what you had previously thought of as a reasonably straightforward task began to look very complex and demanding. You then began to doubt whether you had the ability to be a good preacher. Before long you had convinced yourself that you are not cut out to be a preacher at all. Now all you want to do is to find a face-saving reason to back out of any preaching engagements before things get any worse!

If even a little of this has been happening to you, relax! These are very common reactions to what we have been doing. (Incidentally, the question asked in 2 Corinthians 2:16 and 3:5 shows that even

---

[5]   Sun-Tzu, *The Art of War*, (Camberwell: Penguin, 2009 [ca.500 BC]), p. 17.

apostles can be daunted by such a responsibility.) To preach God's Word does indeed seem to be a very demanding task, requiring tons of both exegetical and speaking ability. But all that it really requires of you is two things: (1) a humble, teachable attitude (see Isaiah 66:2b), and thus a sincere dependence upon God, and (2) the conviction that this matters enough to put lots of blood, sweat and tears into it. Then, armed with this outlook, get as much practice as you can.

You might indeed be only a 'five loaves and two fishes' person (like 99% of your fellow believers!) – but we serve a Lord who can feed thousands with even very meagre offerings that are made available to him. You might feel that you are unimpressive and that your preaching lacks impact – but we serve a Lord who turned the world upside down through just such a preacher (2 Corinthians 10:10; Acts 17:6). You might have a great sense of weakness and inadequacy every time you have to preach – but we serve a Lord whose Word gives sight to the blind and whose grace triumphs through such powerless people (2 Corinthians 4:4-7; 12:9-10).

GOT IT?

i.   Why is it not a good idea to evaluate my preaching as soon as I have done it?

ii.   What standards should we use to evaluate preaching?

iii.   Should I use the same talk more than once?

iv.   What are the 'post-preaching blues'? What is the best way of dealing with them?

8. The Ministry of Preaching

8.1. *The Ministry of Preaching: To get you thinking...*

A holy-minded man of good renown
There was, and poor, the *Parson* to a town,
Yet he was rich in holy thought and work.
He was also a learned man, a clerk,
Who truly knew Christ's gospel and would preach it
Devoutly to parishioners, and teach it...
This noble example to his sheep he gave,
First following the word before he taught it,
And it was from the gospel he had caught it...
Christ and His Twelve Apostles and their lore
He taught, but followed it himself before.

Geoffrey Chaucer, The Canterbury Tales, rev'd ed., p. 32.

...he meant always to preach in a striking manner, so as to have his congregation swelled by admirers from neighbouring parishes, and to produce a great sensation whenever he took occasional duty for a brother clergyman of minor gifts. The style of preaching he had chosen was the extemporaneous, which was held little short of the miraculous in rural parishes...

George Eliot, The Mill on the Floss, p. 134.

O Vanity!...Thou odious, deformed monster! whom priests have railed at, philosophers despised, and poets ridiculed: is there a wretch so abandoned as to own thee for an acquaintance in publick? yet, how few will refuse to enjoy thee in private?...All our passions are thy slaves. Avarice itself is often no more than thy hand-maid, and even Lust thy pimp. The bully Fear like a coward, flies before thee, and Joy and Grief hide their heads in thy presence. I know thou wilt think, that whilst I abuse thee, I court thee...

Henry Fielding, Joseph Andrews, (Penguin Classics), (Harmondsworth: Penguin, 1977
[1742]), p. 83.

O Lord God! give, I beseech you, both now and at all times hereafter to your church pastors and teachers after your own heart, even such as shall bring the sheep of Christ into his fold, and who, through the influence of your good Spirit, shall feed them with saving knowledge and understanding. Make every preacher of your Word know and always remember that neither is he that planteth any thing, neither he that watereth, but you are all in all, who alone can give the increase. Let none of them vainly presume on their skill and ability to do any good by their preaching, and obtain any good success, but let them all humbly wait upon you, and by fervent daily prayer let them seek for and obtain the aids of your grace, to enable them to dispense the word of life, and let your blessing render their preaching happily successful to the souls of those that hear them. Amen.

August H. Francke, 'A Letter to a Friend Concerning the Most Useful Way of Preaching', in Peter C. Erb [ed.] Pietists: Selected Writings, p. 127.

It often surprises us that very young men can muster courage to preach for the first time to a strange congregation. Men who are as yet but little more than boys, who have but just left...a seminary intended for their tuition as scholars, whose thoughts have been mostly of boating, cricketing, and wine parties, ascend a rostrum high above the heads of the submissive crowd...It seems strange to us that they are not stricken dumb by the new and awful solemnity of their position. How am I, just turned twenty-three, who have never yet passed ten thoughtful days since the power of thought first came to me, how am I to instruct these greybeards, who with the weary thinking of so many years have approached so near the grave? Can I teach them their duty? Can I explain to them that which I so imperfectly understand, that which years of study may have made so plain to them? Has my newly acquired privilege, as one of God's ministers, imparted to me as yet any fitness for the wonderful work of a preacher?

Anthony Trollope, Barchester Towers, p. 207.

8.2. The Ministry of Preaching: Guidance from Scripture

I know whom I have believed, and am convinced that he is able to guard what I have entrusted to him until that day.

2 Timothy 1:12.

Therefore, since through God's mercy we have this ministry, we do not lose heart. [2] Rather, we have renounced secret and shameful ways; we do not use deception, nor do we distort the word of God. On the contrary, by setting forth the truth plainly we commend ourselves to everyone's conscience in the sight of God.

2 Corinthians 4:1-2

With this chapter we come full circle, back to where we began. This means that we are going to focus again on know-what and know-why instead of on know-how. So instead of considering problems with our practice, we will be looking at problematic desires and attitudes. And instead of describing specific techniques as solutions, we will be reflecting on fundamental attitudes and commitments that we should have.

8.3. Putting Preaching in its Place

Although we have referred to this matter several times along the way, it is so important that it needs special attention in its own right. I am referring to the preacher's commitment to living with God and for God, and to the place of the Bible and prayer in our day-by-day expression of that commitment.

The first issue we must address here is the necessity of feeding upon the Word and coming to God in prayer every day. If this set of twins is not given priority daily, the inevitable result is that we will not continue to grow as we should 'in the grace and knowledge of our Lord and Saviour Jesus Christ' (2 Peter 3:18).

> Where...personal devotions languish, there professional lusts of pride and self-esteem, of fatigue and busy-ness, begin to flourish unhindered. And then the seed of the Word begins to be choked out of the preacher who forgets that he is not only its sower but

its field.[1]

Neglect of time alone with God is the single greatest spiritual pitfall you and I face.[2]

Secondly, it is essential that I recognize my obligation to grow, so that my study of Scripture and commitment to prayer is aimed at my steady growth in both knowledge and love of God and also godliness and maturity of character.

Cooks who prepare meals for others but rarely take time to feed themselves will eventually suffer from malnutrition.[3]

Thirdly, before I am a preacher I am a child of the Father and a servant of the Master. This means that the attention I give to the Bible and prayer must flow into living for God in all the aspects of everyday life. There must be no divorce between devotion and discipleship, piety and practice.

[We begin the day with prayer.] But have we then done with him for all day? No, we must still be waiting on him; as one to whom we stand very nearly related, and very strongly obliged. To wait on God is to live a life of desire towards him, delight in him, dependence on him, and devotedness to him.[4]

The most important balance we will ever need in expository preaching is that between our own proclamation of divine truth and our own practice of that divine truth.[5]

Fourthly, my commitment to the Bible and prayer must not be limited to my preparation of talks. If this is the only Bible study and praying I do, I am not living each day with God as I should.

...we must constantly beware lest we fall into the habit of reading the Bible only as a perfunctory matter, a professional duty. In the spirit of personal devoutness, with a desire for personal benefit, and with the constant prayer that God would bless us in learning and in teaching, let us study the Bible that

---

[1]   Richard R. Caemmerer, *Preaching for the Church*, p. 261.
[2]   Reid Ferguson, *The Little Book of Things You Should Know about Ministry*, p. 52.
[3]   Warren W. Wiersbe, *The Dynamics of Preaching*, p. 88.
[4]   Matthew Henry, *The Secret of Communion with God*, (Grand Rapids: Kregel, 1991 [1712]), p. 46.
[5]   Derek Newton, *And the Word Became...A Sermon*, p. 259.

we may 'save both ourselves, and them that hear us.'[6]

> Our natural tendency is to become so involved in the exercise of our gifts, talents, and skills in ministry that we neglect or forget about the need to cultivate our heart and soul.[7]

Fifthly, my preparation for preaching must nevertheless involve careful study of and meditation on the Bible, and earnest prayer about every aspect of the great responsibility of bringing God's words to others.

> Whatever it takes, the pastor must have a disciplined habit of personal prayer, in which he prays for himself, his preparations, his pastoring and his preaching.[8]

My most important preparation for preaching, therefore, is what I do when I am not preparing for preaching! The person who goes occasionally to the Bible and to prayer as a preacher should be going to them daily as a believer. Yet we all know how easily our firmest resolutions and disciplines come unstuck in the hustle and bustle of daily life. There is often a sizeable gap between what we know we should do and what we actually do. This is where my need to prepare for preaching can prove to be a blessing rather than a burden, for it can often be the catalyst that succeeds in bringing me to the Bible and prayer. It is most definitely better to read the Bible and pray for this reason than not to do it at all! One of the privileges of being a preacher is having this extra incentive to do what I should be doing anyway.

8.4. Common Problems in Ministry

There are various problems that affect most preachers sooner or later. These are not limited to preachers – but they can impact upon us in ways that are somewhat different from how they affect other Christians. So while books about the Christian life will often deal with the problems we are about to consider, few will look at them from the particular angle the preacher needs. This is what we are going to do now. Once we have worked our way through these problems, we will then examine the attitudes and commitments that provide an antidote to them.

---

[6] John A. Broadus, *On the Preparation and Delivery of Sermons*, p. 79.
[7] Aubrey Malphurs, *The Dynamics of Church Leadership*, (Grand Rapids: Baker, 1999), p. 28.
[8] Murray A. Capill, *Preaching with Spiritual Vigour*, p. 58.

8.4.1. *Busyness*

One of the most difficult aspects of being a preacher is that the job is never finished; there is always more that needs to be done – more of the Bible to be expounded; more of the Bible to be understood so that it can be expounded; more to be learned in those parts of the Bible that have been expounded already; more appropriation of and obedience to what has been preached; another talk to be prepared – and so on...and on. And this is only the 'more' that is directly connected with my preaching – but every preacher has commitments and responsibilities over and above those that come from being a preacher, of course. We are all busy people, and there are times when our busyness threatens to undo our commitment to careful preparation and thoughtful preaching.

> ...pastoring, like parenting, is always a work in progress, an unfinished task...We believe in the work. We want to honour God and to serve people, so we tend to work hard. Of itself, hard work is not a problem; but it can become one if we neglect our families, ignore the physical and emotional strains upon our bodies and minds, and become frantically busy...Only drivenness, with the resultant desire to be seen by people rather than by our gracious God, can account for this mistake [that is, prayerlessness and lack of preaching preparation], with its resultant guilt and energy-sapping lifestyle.[9]

At one level, the problem of busyness is simply the problem of *priorities*. This is always with us – no matter how many times we have faced and resolved the challenges involved, this continues to be a major issue in our lives. And in working out the priorities we should have, all of us have to learn how to live within limits – the limits of our time, our energy, and our abilities. That is, we all have to decide where to draw the line, and which good things will remain undone because we simply cannot fit them in.

> A concert violinist was once asked the secret of her skill, to which she replied 'planned neglect'. She had found that if she did all the things that needed doing she never had time to practice. Now she started with violin practice even if it meant the

---

9   Peter Brain, *Going the Distance: How to Stay Fit for a Lifetime of Ministry*, (Kingsford: Matthias Media, 2004), pp. 12, 18.

neglect of other things. The problem is never lack of time – it is competing priorities.[10]

So if our preaching preparation is always being undermined by our busyness, that can only mean that we are not giving it a high enough priority – or to make the same point another way, we are making other activities a higher priority than our preaching. Such busyness is usually the result of our failure to realize that we must draw a line between the good that must be done and the good that can't be done. Very often, this failure reflects a deeper problem – the lack of a clear sense of my calling; a troubling confusion about what I am. For pastors, this often manifests itself as the tension between time spent with people (in pastoral counselling and the like) and time spent in preparing to preach. To some extent this tension stems from a failure to recognize that faithful preaching of God's Word is a very effective method of pastoring. After all, a clearly explained and sensitively applied expository talk given to a congregation of fifty people represents some twenty-five hours of worthwhile pastoral counselling!

So there is only one way to deal adequately with this issue every time it confronts us. In order to know what I should leave out I have to know what I must give myself to – my 'No' will be an echo of my 'Yes'. (I'm not for a moment suggesting that we must say 'No' to people in order to say 'Yes' to preaching. The issue of priorities is not about choosing one rather than the other, but about striking the right balance between them.)

For some people, however, busyness represents a different kind of problem. For them it is escapism, a form of task-avoidance, an unwillingness to knuckle down and do what should be done.

> Sloth doesn't necessarily mean we're doing nothing. Sloth is the failure to do what needs to be done when it needs to be done – like the kamikaze pilot who flew seventeen missions...even workaholics can be lazy. They may work furiously only because they are trying to avoid doing something truly needful.[11]

This might just be the result of weariness, and a sign that a good break

---

[10]   Tim Chester, *The Message of Prayer*, (Leicester: IVP, 2003), p. 230.
[11]   John Ortberg in Richard Exley, Mark Galli & John Ortberg, *Dangers, Toils and Snares*, (Sisters: Multnomah, 1994), p. 52f.

is overdue. If it is a regular pattern, however, it probably masks a deeper problem – in which case, I need to get the problem uncovered so that I can work at resolving it. It is possible that I will need help to get this done, especially if this pattern has been evident in my life and ministry for some time.

For still others, busyness is the result of a failure to draw the boundary in the right place. They are over-ambitious, unrealistic about what they can manage, so the workload they have accepted is greater than their capacity. If this continues to be an issue, it is time to face the fact that this too is likely to be the symptom of a deeper problem.

So the problem of busyness can prove to be much deeper than simply sorting out our priorities. Too many Christians who hold ministry positions are over busy because they are driven people, driven by needs and desires that they recognize only dimly, if at all. I know, because I was one of them! As I discovered to my astonishment when my drivenness had brought me undone, the only effective antidote is a fresh appropriation of God's grace. Until this became clear to me, I was convinced that I was a sincere, even passionate believer in and teacher of the grace of God. But eventually I came to see that my convictions about grace and my hold upon it were not much more than skin-deep – certainly sincere, but also very shallow. More of this below.

8.4.2. Discouragement

Just occasionally I have thought I could write a book about being a pastor. The book would have three chapters, each considering a key area of the pastor's work: catching fish; feeding sheep – and herding cats! I am joking, of course – but this is a little reminder that there is plenty of opportunity for discouragement in a pastor's work. Much of it can centre on my preaching. I can work hard and faithfully in my preparation; I can give myself in the actual preaching itself – and yet there doesn't seem to be either much growth in the hearers or much appreciation from them. Over time, this discouragement can act like a corrosive acid on my resolutions about doing careful preparation and faithful exposition. I need to know, therefore, what antidotes to apply to it, so that it doesn't undermine my ministry as a preacher. (What these antidotes are we will see below.)

It is easy to become discouraged as a preacher. The pulpit is a lonely and vulnerable place to be. Hard messages are always hard to preach, but they need to be heard. Proper preaching, which involves declaring what God is saying through his Word, is therefore something which requires great courage.[12]

Now we turn our attention to common problems that arise directly out of the fact that the preacher stands up to be seen and heard by a (sometimes quite large) group of people. These are a group of *five peas* – yet they are anything but sweet peas, for they are more like noxious weeds, hard to eradicate and dangerous to be around.

8.4.3. *Pretence*

It is not uncommon for my preaching to deceive my hearers. It is all too easy for them to think that the preacher is more devout and more holy – in short, a better Christian – than they are. This also means that they have come to believe that I am a better Christian than I really am. It is vital for their spiritual health, and mine as well, that I do nothing to foster this tendency. Instead, I should often echo the Psalmist's prayer: 'Keep me from deceitful ways' (Psalm 119:29).

> 'And now to God the Father', he ends,
> And his voice thrills up to the topmost tiles:
> Each listener chokes as he bows and bends,
> And emotion pervades the crowded aisles.
> Then the preacher glides to the vestry-door,
> And shuts it, and thinks he is seen no more.
>
> The door swings softly ajar meanwhile,
> And a pupil of his in the Bible class,
> Who adores him as one without gloss or guile,
> Sees her idol stand with a satisfied smile
> And re-enact at the vestry-glass
> Each pulpit gesture in deft dumb-show
> That had moved the congregation so.[13]

I might not be able to prevent my hearers thinking of me more highly than they should – but I can most certainly prevent myself from acting a part, creating a false ministry persona that obscures the real me from view.

---

[12]   Stephen McQuoid, *The Beginner's Guide to Expository Preaching*, (Fearn: Christian Focus, 2002), p. 43.

[13]   Thomas Hardy, 'Satires of Circumstance, II: In Church' in *Thomas Hardy*, (The Penguin Poets), (Harmondsworth: Penguin, 1960), p. 121.

There is never any justification for this kind of pretence in Christian ministry: 'in Christ we speak before God with sincerity...we have renounced secret and shameful ways; we do not use deception' (2 Corinthians 2:17; 4:2). 1 Thessalonians 2:1-12 is especially important in this regard, and deserves to be read, pondered, and prayed through regularly.

In addition to deceiving other people about my true spiritual condition, it is tragically possible for my preaching to deceive me as well. So unless I am vigilant here, it is quite possible for me to end up amongst the ranks of the 'impostors...deceiving and being deceived' (2 Timothy 3:13). One of the greatest dangers facing me as a preacher is to think that because I have preached about something I have also done it – but a sermon series on prayer is no substitute for a disciplined prayer-life; preaching about forgiveness does not mean that I am a forgiving person; and preaching against sin is not the same as combating my own besetting sins.

8.4.4. Praise

Human beings are the only creatures who can get a swollen head from a pat on the back! Praise is a very seductive and intoxicating brew – so it is not surprising that the Bible tells us that 'a person is tested by being praised'.[14] It is all too easy to become thoroughly addicted to it, even to the point where I go searching for it if it doesn't come. Such a desire for praise means that I crave popularity, the approval of other people.

> ...I know not whether any man ever succeeded in the effort not to be pleased when he is praised, and the man who is pleased at this is likely also to desire to enjoy it, and the man who desires to enjoy it will, of necessity, be altogether vexed and beside himself whenever he misses it...they who long for applause...when they are not constantly being praised, become, as by some famine, wasted in soul...He who enters upon the trial of preaching with desires of this kind, how many annoyances and how many pangs dost thou think that he has? It is no more possible for the sea to be without waves than that man to be without cares and grief.[15]

---

[14]   Proverbs 27:21 NRSV; cf. NASB.

[15]   John Chrysostom, *On the Priesthood*, V.4, 7 (NPNF IX, 1st Series), (Edinburgh: T & T Clark/ Grand Rapids: Eerdmans, 1989 [ca.390]), pp. 71, 73.

[I was a new Christian speaking to 20,000 pastors.] When I finished I...folded up my notes and walked away. Suddenly there was a deafening sound...I saw people standing on their feet...I stood in the middle of the platform dumbfounded. Brother Blow threw his arms around me and even in that moment of joy ministered to me just as faithfully as he did in prison. 'Careful, boy,' he whispered, 'Satan is on your back.' To this day, I hear his words rising over any applause I receive when speaking.[16]

If praise has the potential to feed my pride and so to cause much damage, what should I do when people thank me for a talk I have given and say how good they thought it was? Since such words of appreciation are usually meant to encourage me, I should neither reject them nor wallow in them. On the one hand, it would simply be rude to dismiss people's words of thanks, as though they had committed some offence by uttering them. But on the other hand, I don't need to do any more than respond with a smile and a simple 'Thank you' of my own. If my congratulators keep adding to their original thanks, I can often respond with a comment like, 'Yes, it's a great passage, isn't it?'—shifting the focus away from me and putting it where it really belongs.

8.4.5. *Popularity*

Popularity is praise that keeps coming, approval that lasts. This is dangerous for me as a preacher, especially if it feeds my sense of self-worth. Then I am likely to avoid saying anything that risks making me unpopular – however much the Bible insists on it. At this point, of course, my desire for popularity with my hearers has become the enemy of my faithfulness to God.

> Beware, I beg you, of the temptation to be a popular preacher! I doubt if it is possible to be popular and faithful at the same time. Either we go for popularity at the expense of faithfulness, or we are determined to be faithful even at the expense of popularity. If we compromised less, we would undoubtedly suffer more. For the cross is still foolishness to some and a stumbling-block to others.[17]

---

[16] Charles W. Colson, *Life Sentence*, (Minneapolis: World Wide, 1979), p. 38f.
[17] John Stott, *Calling Christian Leaders*, (Leicester: IVP, 2002), p. 124.

...our message remains the simple and foolish message of the cross. We have no other message to offer the world, and if we try to attract the world by offering something more sophisticated or appealing we will be way off target...We cannot expect, of course, that such a foolish message will be widely welcomed. It takes courage to speak as a fool in a world which prizes its own misguided wisdom.[18]

This is an issue that I must settle from the beginning – and must keep coming back to so that it does not bring me undone. It really is impossible to serve two masters (Matthew 6:24), so I must choose constantly to give my loyalty to God and his Word of truth. This means choosing to turn a deaf ear to the applause and approval of other people, as the Bible clearly indicates: 'Am I now trying to win human approval, or God's approval? Or am I trying to please people? If I were still trying to please people I would not be a servant of Christ.' (Galatians 1:10).

Paul aimed to preach not that which was pleasing, but that which was profitable, and to please only in order to profit.[19]

I do not mean that nobody will thank me for being true to God and his Word in my preaching, for his sheep really do listen to his voice and follow him (John 10:2-5, 27). But I will always win more plaudits by being in tune with the popular mood than by 'marching to the beat of a different drummer'. The issue here is what my heart is set on – popular approval or pleasing God.

Although it is no longer customary to show approval by this means, the essential problem we face is no different from the long-gone era when hearers applauded whenever they approved what the preacher was saying – as this quotation from the end of the 4th century shows.

Many take a deal of pains to be able to stand up in public, and make a long speech: and if they get applause from the multitude, it is to them as if they gained the very kingdom: but if silence follows the close of their speech, it is worse than hell itself, the dejection that falls upon their spirits from the silence! This has turned the Churches upside down...when we idly busy

---

18   Derek Tidball, *Builders and Fools*, (Leicester: IVP, 1999), p. 77.

19   Matthew Henry, *Commentary on the Whole Bible*, (Peabody: Hendrickson, 2008 [1706-14]), p. 1724 (on Acts 20:20).

ourselves about beautiful expressions, and the composition and harmony of our sentences, in order that we may please, not profit: we make it our aim to be admired, not to instruct; to delight, not prick to the heart; to be applauded and depart with praise, not to correct men's manners!...often I have thought to make a rule which should prevent all applauding, and persuade you to listen with silence and becoming orderliness...Nothing so becomes a Church as silence and good order. Noise belongs to theatres, and baths, and public processions, and market places: but where doctrines, and such doctrines, are the subject of teaching, there should be stillness, and quiet, and calm reflection...[20]

8.4.6. Power

There is often a very fine line between wanting my preaching to have its rightful effect on the hearers and wanting to exercise power over them by my preaching. Ironically, this problem can be compounded when I work hard at preaching as well as I possibly can. The more they appreciate my preaching, the more influence my hearers will give it – and therefore me – in their lives. It is all too easy to abuse this trust. One way in which this can happen is that I move from forceful preaching – preaching that wants the hearers to be gripped and moved by the truths of Scripture, as they should be – into browbeating and even bullying, attempting to dominate the hearers. This is where I use words as weapons with which I impose myself on the hearers and whip them into shape.

> I'd get the upper hand of those savages like a strong sun. Strong, yes, that was the word I constantly had on the tip of my tongue, I dreamed of absolute power, the kind that makes people kneel down, that forces the adversary to capitulate, converts him in short, and the blinder, the crueler he is, the more he's sure of himself, mired in his own conviction, the more his consent establishes the royalty of whoever brought about his collapse. Converting good folk who had strayed somewhat was the shabby ideal of our priests, I despised them

---

[20] John Chrysostom, *Homily XXX on the Acts of the Apostles*, (NPNF XI, 1st series (Edinburgh: T & T Clark/ Grand Rapids: Eerdmans, 1989 [400]), pp. 193-4.

for daring so little when they could do so much, they lacked faith and I had it, I wanted to be acknowledge by the torturers themselves, to fling them on their knees and make them say: 'O Lord, here is thy victory,' to rule in short by the sheer force of words over an army of the wicked.[21]

The Bible is very clear about this – lording it over others is never justifiable, and thus never acceptable for the preacher: 'You know that those who are regarded as rulers of the Gentiles lord it over them...Not so with you. Instead, whoever wants to become great among you must be your servant' (Mark 10:42-43).

This means that the only power I should seek as a preacher is that the message I am privileged to expound will impact the hearers as powerfully as possible, to give new depth and direction to their lives. All of my powers – whatever gifts I have – must be consecrated to this one great goal. Where power is concerned, my sole focus should be the power of the Word in the ministry of the Spirit.

> It seems that the only preaching God honours, through which His wisdom and power are expressed, is the preaching of a man who is willing in himself to be both a weakling and a fool. God not only chooses weak and foolish people to save, but weak and foolish preachers through whom to save them, or at least preachers who are content to be weak and seem foolish in the eyes of the world. We are not always willing to pay this price.[22]

> ...power is safe only in the hands of those who humble themselves to serve.[23]

8.4.7. Pride

This is the poison that makes the previous peas so damaging, the evil energy that feeds all of these other errors and uses them to wreak havoc in my soul and in my ministry. This is why I am tempted to act a part, why I love to be praised, why I long to be popular, why I want to be in

---

[21]   Albert Camus, 'The Renegade' in *Exile and the Kingdom*, (Harmondsworth: Penguin, 1962), p. 33f.

[22]   John R. W. Stott, *The Preacher's Portrait*, p. 109. He is referring to 1 Corinthians 2:1-5 in particular.

[23]   John Stott, *New Issues Facing Christians Today*, 3rd ed., (London: Marshall Pickering, 1999), p. 431.

control. In a very real sense, then, being a preacher puts me in a dangerous position because it puts these sins within my reach.

> Pride is the beginning of sin, the first impulse and movement toward evil...For every sin begins from it, and is maintained by it...From pride springs contempt of the poor, desire of riches, the love of power, the longing for much glory...There is therefore no evil like pride.[24]

> ...it is the special danger of ministers to have high opinions of themselves because of the high dignity of their service.[25]

> It is certain that a young man who fervently loves God, although adorned with limited gifts, will be more useful to the church of God with his meager talent and academic achievement than a vain and worldly fool with double doctor's degrees who is very clever but has not been taught by God.[26]

> Pride is without doubt the chief occupational hazard of the preacher. It has ruined many, and deprived their ministry of power...We need to cry out with Baxter, 'O what a constant companion, what a tyrannical commander, what a sly, subtle and insinuating enemy is this sin of pride!'[27]

Pride treats others as little more than a means to my ends – so love for others shuts out pride.[28] Worse still, pride would dethrone God and put myself at the centre. It is not surprising, then, that on the day of the Lord judgment will be directed first and foremost at human pride.[29] The Bible makes it clear that pride is synonymous with wickedness and the opposite of faithfulness to God.[30] So pride is one of the distinguishing marks of false teachers, while on the other hand, it is not to characterize

---

[24] John Chrysostom, *Homily I on 2 Thessalonians,* (NPNF XIII, 1st series (Edinburgh: T & T Clark/ Grand Rapids: Eerdmans, 1994 [ca.400]), p. 378.

[25] William Perkins, 'The Calling of the Ministry' in *The Art of Prophesying,* p. 128.

[26] Philip J. Spener, *Pia Desideria,* translated, edited, and with an Introduction by T. G. Tappert (Philadelphia: Fortress, 1964 [1675]), p. 108.

[27] John Stott, *I Believe in Preaching,* pp. 320-1. (The quotation is from Richard Baxter, *The Reformed Pastor,* p. 137.)

[28] See Romans 12:9, 16; 1 Corinthians 13:4; Philippians 2:1-4; cf. 2 Timothy 3:2.

[29] See Isaiah 2:10-18; 13:6-13; cf. Job 40:11-12; Proverbs 15:25; 16:5.

[30] See Psalms 31:23; 94:2-3; 101:5-6; Proverbs 21:4.

God's servants.[31] We preachers must never forget that 'God opposes the proud'.[32]

> One of our most heinous and palpable sins is *pride*...the sum of all is this, it maketh men, both in studying and preaching, to seek themselves and deny God, when they should seek God's glory and deny themselves. When they should inquire, What shall I say, and how shall I say it, to please God best, and do most good? It makes them ask, What shall I say, and how shall I deliver it, to be thought a learned able preacher, and to be applauded by all that hear me?[33]

I must be vigilant against my pride long before I ever get up to speak. That is because it can corrupt the preparation of my talks, and exercise illegitimate control over what I decide to say and how I decide to say it.

> ...we must be prepared to crucify all that is proud in our sermons. We ought to scrutinize them and remove...anything that is included chiefly for the display of our own abilities. Purge your sermons of words, phrases and illustrations that are included for cleverness' sake.[34]

I must continue to be vigilant against pride while I am speaking and after I have given my talk. Being seen and heard by a group of people is heady wine, and it is all too easy for preachers to become vain. This is easy enough when I preach only occasionally; it is alarmingly easy when I preach regularly.

> Every preacher knows the insidious temptation to vainglory to which the pulpit exposes him. We stand there in a prominent position, lifted above the congregation, the focus of their gaze and the object of their attention. It is a perilous position indeed.[35]

One of God's mercies to the preacher tempted by vanity is so to arrange things that the 'law of the opposite outcome' frequently

---

[31] See 2 Corinthians 11:20 NRSV; 1 Timothy 6:3-5; 2 Peter 2:10, 18; Jude 16; 3 John 9-10; Romans 12:3; Galatians 5:26; Philippians 2:3; Titus 1:7 NRSV.
[32] James 4:6; 1 Peter 5:5; cf. Luke 1:51-52.
[33] Richard Baxter, *The Reformed Pastor*, pp. 137, 138.
[34] Murray A. Capill, *Preaching with Spiritual Vigour*, p. 175.
[35] John R. W. Stott, *The Preacher's Portrait*, p. 69.

applies. When I have given what I thought was an A-grade talk, it often seems to have had no effect; conversely, when I have preached an absolute shocker, people tell me for weeks afterwards how helpful it was! Allied to this is the 'law of the unplanned benefit', when what people remember best and find most helpful in a talk is something that I hadn't planned to say; it just popped out – and sometimes I have absolutely no recollection of having said it at all.

> ...a word cast in by the by hath done more execution in a sermon than all that was spoken besides; sometimes also when I have thought I did no good, then I did most of all, and at other times when I thought I should catch them, I have fished for nothing.[36]

Another mercy is when God enables us to see more of our sin – and thus dents our pride. Pride cannot flourish when I am well aware that I am not worthy to preach God's Word to others:

> I am both foul and brittle; much unfit to deal in holy Writ.[37]

One of my earliest and most vivid experiences of this kind was when I realized how vain I had become in my up-front role as a young preacher. I often prayed earnestly that God would remove this vanity and make me truly humble. It was as I was doing so one day that it suddenly dawned on me that every time I made this request of God I had a mental picture of people discussing amongst themselves how humble I was! I still wanted to be in the centre of attention – if not as an able preacher, then as a humble preacher. In the face of a sin that simply burrows deeper when confronted at any level, God is being merciful to us whenever he shows us that we have no room for smugness and self-satisfaction.

These are not the only problems that affect my preaching, of course. However, those we have looked at give a sufficient indication of their range and types so that we can now consider how to combat such problems.

---

[36] John Bunyan, *Grace Abounding to the Chief of Sinners*, (Penguin Classics), (London: Penguin, 1987 [1666]), p. 72.

[37] George Herbert, 'Priesthood' in *The Poems of George Herbert*, (The World's Classics), (London: OUP, 1961), p. 151.

8.5.   Antidotes to Ministry Problems

Just as we did with the problems we have just examined, we will look at these antidotes – for the most part, basic characteristics of the Christian life – from the perspective of the preacher. The best way to use the following material is to consider how each of these 'antidotes' applies to one or more of the problems we have just considered – problems that you might be facing already. So where should we begin? As with everything else Christian, with the grace of God.

8.5.1.   Privilege

All Christian service is a privilege. It is not just Paul, but every one of us, who should acknowledge that 'through God's mercy we have this ministry' (2 Corinthians 4:1). The fact is that God does not need us – he made the cosmos without any help from us, and he could also save the world without our help. Yet he chooses to make room for us, to give us a place in his work. In doing so he confers upon us the great dignity of being his co-workers.[38]

> Would that the many who have regular opportunity as Christians to preach and to teach could be made to feel the amazing wonder of their high privilege, and the full burden of their solemn responsibility, as ministers of the God-given Word. Then they would unquestionably give a new priority to the worthy discharge of their stewardship.[39]

As a result, all of us can and should echo Paul in acknowledging that 'by the grace of God I am what I am' (1 Corinthians 15:10). So in all of our ministries, whatever they are, we are called to be 'faithful stewards of God's grace' (1 Peter 4:10). This certainly applies to preaching, whether we do it weekly or only occasionally.

If what we might call God's serving grace makes me what I am, there is a deeper sense in which this is true of God's saving grace. It is not only what I am in my ministry but what I am in my identity that is due to the grace of God. Out of his grace God has conferred upon us a new status and identity as his adopted, freed, reconciled children, who

---

[38]   See 1 Corinthians 3:9; 2 Corinthians 6:1; 1 Thessalonians 3:2.
[39]   Alan M. Stibbs, *Expounding God's Word*, (London: IVF, 1960), p. 14.

have been put right with him and given a secure and eternal place in his salvation. It is what I am and have because of this grace that provides the strongest and most effective antidote against the problems that can otherwise beset me. A deeper understanding and appropriation of the grace of God – his love that is always rich and free – is the pathway to a life and ministry that is rich and free.

> If your joy and identity are found in ministry, then ministry will crush you. But if you live within the grace of God...then you can embrace this as the good life.[40]

It is here that I must fight the battle against compulsive busyness and what drives me to it, against the need for praise and power, against pretence and pride. It is only when I have a secure sense of who I am before God that I have an antidote strong enough to sever these problems at the root.

> Justification by faith keeps us from the need for self-justification, or the need always to be noticed or praised by others. As such, it is a powerful remedy to self-delusion and despair. If I am always dependent upon the assessment of others for approval...chances are I will put my energies into work that will win the most approval and applause. In so doing, I will be failing to do the real work of pastoring, and even what real work of pastoring I do will be done from improper motives. Justification by faith will provide me with the glue that will enable me to stick to my real tasks, seeking the approval of the One who really counts.[41]

8.5.2. Faithfulness

Since our ministry as preachers is a huge privilege, our chief responsibility is to be faithful in the way we exercise it. One of the ways the New Testament applies this to our preaching is by using the image of the steward, the servant whose master entrusts him with important responsibilities. The steward's overriding responsibility is to be faithful to the master by doing what he has been commissioned to do: 'those who have been given a trust must prove faithful' (1 Corinthians 4:2). As

---

[40]   Tim Chester, *The Ordinary Hero: Living the Cross and Resurrection*, (Nottingham: IVP, 2009), p. 89f.

[41]   Peter Brain, *Going the Distance: How to Stay Fit for a Lifetime of Ministry*, p. 250.

preachers we have been entrusted with a great task, so we must set ourselves to be trustworthy – true to our Master, true to the message, and true to the task of making it known.[42]

> Your ultimate concern is not what people say or what they think. You don't care what the climate of the market is, or what people say they want. You have a higher calling than felt-need sermonizing that aims at satisfying the customer. Your call is to please the Creator of heaven and earth, the Lord of lords. Your summons is to faithful stewardship. Your vocation is to declare and teach the powerful content of the whole counsel of God.[43]

The steward does not aim to be successful but to be faithful – or rather, his faithfulness is his success. The only commendation that counts in the end will not be, 'Well done, good and successful servant.' So as preachers we have succeeded not when our hearers approve of what we say, or when their ranks swell, or when we get a reputation for being 'a good preacher', but when we have delivered God's message faithfully.

8.5.3.   Integrity

One of the principal ingredients of faithfulness is integrity, a thoroughgoing consistency between what we say and what we do and what we are. While this should characterize every believer, it is especially required in the preacher.[44]

It is important to get the balance right here. Integrity means that there should be no discrepancy between my preaching and my life as a believer – but preaching systematically through sections of the Bible will inevitably involve speaking about matters that are outside my experience. This is not necessarily a contradiction, for my integrity is compromised when my preaching and my life are pointing in opposite directions, not when my preaching points beyond where I have got to in the life of faith. Integrity does not require that I have no more growing to do; it does require that my life is moving in the direction to which my preaching points.

---

[42]   See Matthew 25:14-23; 1 Corinthians 4:1-5; 1 Timothy 1:12; 6:20; 2 Timothy 1:14; 2:2, 15; Titus 1:7-9.

[43]   David Eby, *Power Preaching for Church Growth*, (Fearn: Mentor, 1996), p. 63f.

[44]   See 2 Corinthians 2:17; 4:2; 6:6-10; 1 Thessalonians 2:3-12; 1 Timothy 3:2-13; 4:12; 5:21-22; 2 Timothy 2:21-25; Titus 1:6-9; 2:7-8; James 3:1-2; 1 Peter 5:2-3.

> The most important balance we will ever need in expository preaching is that between our own proclamation of divine truth and our own practice of that divine truth.[45]

Because integrity is so vitally important, the lack of it can cripple my preaching ministry. People will be understandably reluctant to be taught by those who appear to be hypocrites, whose practice bears no discernible relation to their preaching. So if my life makes my words sound hollow, sooner or later people will stop their ears – or they will simply stop coming to hear me preach.

> Sincerity, consistency and reliability: failure to demonstrate integrity in these ways is quite possibly the most serious obstacle in any form of Christian ministry and, indeed, in the growth of God's work.[46]

8.5.4. Perseverance

Another dimension of faithfulness is perseverance, the stickability which endures and does not give up. This is where the battle against discouragement is fought. If discouragement is essentially a loss of hope, its chief counterpart is endurance or perseverance, one of the principal expressions of hope.[47] Again, while this should characterize every believer,[48] there are particular ways in which it is required of the preacher.[49]

Perhaps the principal way in which the preacher needs to be persevering is in continuing to put lots of time and effort into preparation, especially when there doesn't appear to be any significant growth in the hearers. This is when my convictions are put to the test – do I really believe that God uses his Word to do his work in people's lives? Do I really believe Isaiah 55:10-11? If so, I will do all that I can to be a faithful steward who sticks at the task assigned by the Master.

> ...the power of unbelief will be a matter of daily conflict to the end...It will induce a faintness under want of success, or self-

---

[45] Derek Newton, *And the Word Became...A Sermon*, p. 259.

[46] Jonathan Lamb, *Integrity: Leading with God Watching*, (Nottingham: IVP, 2006), p. 34.

[47] See 1 Thessalonians 1:3; Hebrews 10:35-36; 11:26-27.

[48] See Matthew 24:13; Romans 5:3-4; 8:25; Galatians 6:9; Colossians 1:11; 1 Thessalonians 1:4; Hebrews 12:1-3; James 1:3-4; 2 Peter 1:6; Revelation 1:9; 13:10; 14:12.

[49] See 2 Corinthians 4:1, 16-18; 6:4; 1 Timothy 4:15-16; 6:11-16; 2 Timothy 3:10, 14; 4:2, 5.

confidence under apparent usefulness; in either case inverting the Scripture order of life and comfort, and leading us to 'walk' by sight, not 'by faith'...[50]

...it is of no slight importance for you to be cleansed of your blind love of self that you may be made more nearly aware of your incapacity; to feel your own incapacity that you may learn to distrust yourself; to distrust yourself that you may transfer your trust to God; to rest with a trustful heart in God that, relying upon his help, you may persevere unconquered to the end...[51]

...the true usefulness of our preaching will not be known to us until each fruit on all the branches on all the trees that have sprung up from all the seeds we've sown has fully ripened in the sunshine of eternity.[52]

Working with human beings, albeit redeemed human beings, brings its fair share of discouragements, setbacks, difficulties and pressures. Sometimes these trip us up. The answer, when they do, is to pick ourselves up, learn from the experience..., and get back in the race.[53]

8.5.5. *Responsible dependence*

Being faithful also means being reliable – and reliable servants of God are reliant people; we depend upon God to do his work with us and through us.[54] This basic expression of faith differs from irresponsible dependence on the one hand and independent responsibility on the other. The first of these expects God to do everything without me, while the second is where I do everything without God. Both rest on the same mistake, which sees God's activity and mine as mutually exclusive, rivals rather than partners. But while God can and often does work without us, he also works with us. According to the Bible, whatever is truly done for him is done with him and through him – he

---

[50] Charles Bridges, *The Christian Ministry*, p. 181.
[51] John Calvin, *Institutes of the Christian Religion*, 1.704.
[52] John Piper, *The Supremacy of God in Preaching*, (Leicester: IVP, 1990), p. 18.
[53] Derek Tidball, *Builders and Fools*, p. 47.
[54] Note especially the following examples: 2 Samuel 10:9-12; Nehemiah 4:9; Psalm 127:1; Colossians 1:29; 2 Timothy 2:7.

works in our working: 'continue to work out your salvation...for it is God who works in you to will and to act in order to fulfil his good purpose.' (Philippians 2:13).

We ought to practise responsible dependence upon God in every aspect of our preaching – the preparation, the delivery, and the outcome.

> Our whole work must be carried on under a deep sense of our own insufficiency, and of our entire dependence on Christ. We must go for light, and life, and strength to him who sends us to the work.[55]

> All through history God has chosen and used nobodies, because their unusual dependence on him made possible the unique display of his grace and power. He chose and used somebodies only when they renounced dependence on their natural abilities and resources.[56]

> ...your job is to faithfully expound the Word...Faithful preaching can bring a small or a large harvest. It is not in your hands to determine the size of the harvest. That's God's prerogative...When there is little or no visible response to your preaching, God's government is the tonic that prevents despondency...And for those few preachers called to preach to many, God's dominion is the antibiotic that drives away the infection of self-dependence, self-congratulation and arrogance...When the ground is hard and frozen, when the seed appears to bounce and never penetrate, when germination seems non-existent, God's sovereignty is the incentive to persevere. God may yet call many who are 'far off'. And when the Lord's mercy is pouring out an abundant harvest, God's sovereignty is the basis for humble worship and joyful adoration...It is this perspective that can keep you on track...And it is this viewpoint alone that can enflame your heart with the seemingly opposite traits of boldness and humility.[57]

The basic reason a minister must pray is not because he is a

---

[55]   Richard Baxter, *The Reformed Pastor*, p. 122.

[56]   Oswald Chambers, quoted in Kent & Barbara Hughes, *Liberating Ministry from the Success Syndrome*, (Wheaton: Tyndale House, 1988), p. 134.

[57]   David Eby, *Power Preaching for Church Growth*, pp. 119, 121.

minister..., but because he is a poor, needy creature dependent on God's grace.[58]

Sadly, it is all too easy to rely upon our preparation rather than upon God. This applies to the preparation we put into each talk we give. We can feel confident as we come to preach because the preparation went well and we are pleased with the resulting talk. Instead, our confidence should be in the fact that God's Spirit will use God's Word to do God's work in our hearers' lives.

> ...any effective ministry of exposition must include both a resolute commitment to the practice of diligent exegesis and a thoroughgoing dependence upon the ministry of the Holy Spirit.
>
> The issue for the preacher is not study or the Spirit, as though a wedge can be driven between the two. It is study and the Spirit. To be sure, study without prayer is atheism. It is a denial of the need of the Spirit's intervention for spiritual understanding. But prayer without study is presumption. It is the resting of confidence on a hope never given by God.[59]
>
> The preacher has no right to rely on the Holy Spirit in matters for which he is responsible, without making any effort himself. With all modesty and earnestness he must labour and strive to present the Word aright, even though he is fully aware that only the Holy Spirit can in fact 'teach aright'.[60]
>
> You have finished your preparation and feel that you have a good sermon, and so you tend to put your reliance on that. There is no greater danger connected with preaching than just that.[61]

The same problem will often apply to the ways in which we prepare ourselves to be better as preachers – we can put our confidence in our training rather than in God, whether this is theological training in general or training in writing and giving talks in particular. While it is right for us to take advantage of every opportunity to improve our

---

[58] James S. Stewart, *Heralds of God*, p. 201.
[59] Arturo Azurdia III, *Spirit Empowered Preaching*, (Fearn: Mentor, 1998), pp. 14, 141.
[60] Karl Barth, *Prayer and Preaching*, (London: SCM, 1964), p. 83.
[61] Martyn Lloyd-Jones, *Preaching and Preachers*, p. 254.

preaching, and right to put as much effort as we can into becoming better preachers, it is not right to do these things without God. We are meant to be both responsible and dependent, working hard while relying on God.

8.5.6. Humble service

Like all other believers, we are meant to be more and more like Jesus. One of the most obvious implications of this is that whatever else preachers are or become, we must never cease being humble servants.[62] Although our ministry puts us out in front of people, our rightful place is not at the top but at the bottom.

> Humility is not a mere ornament of a Christian, but an essential part of the new creature. It is a contradiction in terms, to be a Christian, and not humble...Can we behold him washing and wiping his servants' feet, and yet be proud and lordly still?[63]

> The race is not to the top, where the power and prestige are. The race, for followers of Jesus, is to the bottom where humility, surrender and service are to be found.[64]

> Faith sets the crown on the right head.[65]

> The mark of the true servant of God is a towel and not a scepter. He serves Christ by serving his people.[66]

This must show itself in our preaching – and there are several ways in which this will happen. One is my perseverance in preparing and preaching the best talks I can give. In particular, I will work hard to make the message as clear and easy to understand as possible. Another is my faithfulness in delivering the message of Scripture, whether or not it is palatable, and whether or not I have yet absorbed it fully and integrated it thoroughly within my own devotion and discipleship. Yet another is setting myself steadfastly against pride and all of its perverse

---

[62] See Luke 17:7-10; 22:24-27; John 13:1-17; 1 Corinthians 3:5-7; Philippians 2:3-11; 1 Peter 4:10-11; 5:3-5.

[63] Richard Baxter, *The Reformed Pastor*, p. 143.

[64] Brian J. Dodd, *Empowered Church Leadership*, (Downers Grove: IVP, 2003), p. 142.

[65] Charles H. Spurgeon, *All of Grace*, (Springdale: Whitaker House, 1981), p. 64.

[66] Warren W. and David W. Wiersbe, *Ten Power Principles for Christian Service*, (Grand Rapids: Baker, 1997), p. 36.

offspring. I will also preach as someone who is deeply committed to receiving and responding to whatever the Bible teaches – and not as someone who thinks it applies only to my hearers.

> ...if the first duty of a pastor is to be instructed in the knowledge of sound doctrine, and the second to hold fast his confession with unwavering courage, the third is that he should adapt the method of his teaching to edification and not, out of ambition, fly about among the subtleties of frivolous curiosity, but rather seek only the solid advantage of the Church.[67]

> No man can bear witness to Christ and to himself at the same time...No man can give the impression that he is clever and that Christ is mighty to save.[68]

8.5.7. *Sacrificial commitment*

Becoming more and more like Jesus means following him in the way of the cross – as he gave himself for us, so we are to give ourselves to him and for him.[69] While this should be true in every aspect of our lives, it must especially be true of our ministries.

> ...the way of the cross, and especially the love demonstrated in the cross, is the essential mark of Christian discipleship under the lordship of Christ...It is characterized by sacrifice, submission, self-denial, service and suffering.[70]

> No ministry is worth anything at all which is not first and last and all the time a ministry beneath the Cross.[71]

> The cross is not only something we preach, it is something we live...Paul's own ministry was constantly marked by suffering, frustration and pain. Far from seeking to be free from these, so that he could glide from one triumph and success to another, he interpreted it as a sign of the genuineness of his ministry.

---

[67] John Calvin, *Calvin's NT Commentaries*, 10.361 (on Titus 1:9).

[68] James Denney, *Studies in Theology*, (London: Hodder & Stoughton, 1895), p. 161.

[69] See Matthew 10:24-25; 16:24-25; 20:25-28; John 12:24-26; 15:18-21; Acts 20:22-24, 33-35; 1 Corinthians 4:9-13; 9:3-18, 24-27; 2 Corinthians 5:14-15; 6:3-10; 11:23-29; Philippians 1:21-26; Colossians 1:28-2:1; 4:12-13; 1 Thessalonians 2:8-9; 2 Thessalonians 3:7-9; 2 Timothy 1:8; 2:3, 9-10; 3:10-12.

[70] Tim Chester, *The Ordinary Hero: Living the Cross and Resurrection*, p. 56.

[71] James Stewart, *Heralds of God*, p. 200.

Some seek a ministry without cost. But [this] is a sheer illusion...The costs may differ from time to time and place to place. Most pay the cost of working long and unsociable hours, of being vulnerable, of being weak, of facing criticism, of being lonely, of being drained by people. Ministry takes it out of you...Paying the cost is...what Jesus did and what he calls us to do too.[72]

Christ gave himself up to death on our behalf and became ours: therefore we ought to give up ourselves for the good of all men, not thinking that we are our own, but that we belong to others. For we are not born to live to ourselves...[73]

Our readiness to sacrifice self-interest must characterise our whole approach to preaching. This will mean doing the 'hard yards', not sparing myself as I put in the time and effort my preparation and preaching require. This will involve sacrificing otherwise desirable activities to ensure that I have sufficient time on my own to do my preparation with as much care as it requires. It will also mean exposing myself and my preaching to constructive criticism, so that I can learn and grow as a preacher. It might take the form of personal disciplines that we adopt for the sake of our preaching – for example, choosing to forego otherwise legitimate entertainments on Saturday nights in order to ensure a good night's sleep before Sunday morning's preaching. It might mean a willingness to endure unfriendly criticism as the price we pay for faithfully communicating truths that are biblical but uncomfortable or unpopular.

Our preaching of God's Word will be demanding. It will involve considerable cost and self-denying sacrifice. It will demand our time...preaching will demand self-discipline if we are to give it the effort and energy it deserves. Preaching will demand not only our physical resources but our willingness to think, sometimes long and hard, about sermon preparation and delivery. Not only this, but preaching will demand that we match the words of our lips with the walk and witness of our daily living.[74]

---

[72] Derek Tidball, *Builders and Fools*, pp. 66, 148.
[73] Ulrich Zwingli, 'Of the Education of Youth' in G. W. Bromiley [ed.], *Zwingli and Bullinger*, p. 113.
[74] Derek Newton, *And the Word Became...A Sermon*, p. 8.

If any man will preach as he should preach, his work will take more out of him than any other labour under heaven. If you and I attend to our work and calling, even among a few people, it will certainly produce a friction of soul and a wear of heart which will tell upon the strongest.[75]

8.5.8. Love

Also essential to being like Jesus is self-giving, other-centred love.[76] In addition to seeking to glorify God, this should be the chief motivation of all the effort I put into my preaching. This effort will be a measure of my love for those to whom I preach God's Word, as I will want them to grasp and be grasped by its message. This love will also be reflected in the way that I preach. I will speak as a friend who desires the very best for them, not as a remote figure making a broadcast in their direction – and certainly not as a bully seeking to bring them into subjection. I still shudder at the memory of the street preacher who presented the gospel as though he was absolutely furious with the hearers. I couldn't see then, and I can't see now, how a man who looked and sounded that angry could convince anyone about an amazingly loving God.

> To be servants of the Word it is not enough to love preaching; we have to love people. To love preaching means that we are loving our own actions...To call it a ministry is a deception, because we are not ministering or serving anyone but ourselves and our sense of achievement...Our ministry is a means to an end, and its only value lies in the extent to which it serves the people who hear us.[77]

> In order to defend truth, it is necessary to imbue it with love; in order to teach one must love, for he who feels that he is loved is in a better position to understand.[78]

---

[75]   Charles H Spurgeon, *An All-Round Ministry*, p. 134.
[76]   See John 10:11-18; 13:1, 12-17; 15:9-10; 1 Corinthians 12:27–14:5; Philippians 2:1-8; 4:1; 1 Thessalonians 2:7-8; 3:12; 1 Timothy 4:12; 6:11; 2 Timothy 2:22-25; 1 John 2:6-11; 3:11-18; 4:7-12.
[77]   Peter Adam, *Speaking God's Words*, p. 163.
[78]   Franz J. Leenhardt, *The Epistle to the Romans*, (London: Lutterworth, 1961), p. 354 (on 14:16).

Love of the truth which is not accompanied by love for others brings no honour to God...[79]

...our love for saints and sinners must be governed by our love for God and his truth. Why? Because in Christian service we constantly face the danger of our hearts becoming marshmallows and our spines becoming spaghetti, and what ought to be strong love gradually becomes shallow sentiment.[80]

GOT IT?

i.   What is the most important preparation I do for preaching?

ii.   What problems might underlie the problem of busyness?

iii. What are the five problem peas?

iv.   What is the most important antidote against problems in my ministry?

v.   How will being like Jesus show itself in our ministries?

---

[79] Iain H. Murray, *Spurgeon v. Hyper-Calvinism: The Battle for Gospel Preaching*, (Edinburgh: Banner of Truth, 1995), p. xv.

[80] Warren W. and David W. Wiersbe, *Ten Power Principles for Christian Service*, p. 44.

Conclusion

This will not be like the conclusion to one of my talks – I am not going to repeat the main points, and I am not going to urge you to respond in particular ways to what I have said. Instead, I have only a few brief comments to make.

First, while I hope you will learn good things from this book, it is important that you filter out what is me and not you. What you need to be is the best preacher you can be – not a preacher who is just like me!

Secondly, I hope you are not disappointed to find that I have not included a completed talk on Matthew 6:5-13. This omission is deliberate, because I don't want you to give my talks; I want you to give yours! The work we have done on the passage has been intended to stimulate and assist you in your own talk preparation, whether or not that includes one on this passage. If this has been your aim, and if you have joined me in doing the work along the way, you will find that you are not very far from having a talk you can deliver. I hope you will keep going, to complete your preparation and then to give the talk.

Thirdly, if you have realized that preaching is not for you, let me encourage you to give this book to someone who is or should be a preacher. Why do I say this? Because I am certain that faithful biblical preaching is important – and also, in our desperately lost world, sorely needed. If this book encourages just a few to give themselves to this vital ministry, I will be more than content.

So finally, if you are a preacher, I hope that what you find in this book will strengthen your resolve to keep putting your very best into your preaching – whether you are just beginning, or whether you have been preaching for years; whether you are full of enthusiasm, or whether you are weary and in something of a rut. More than that, I hope that this book will inspire in you the confidence that God will be pleased to use your less-than-perfect efforts to do his wonderful work in people's lives.

> If you speak, you should do so as one who speaks the very words of God...so that in all things God may be praised through Jesus Christ. To him be the glory and the power for ever and ever. Amen.

1 Peter 4:11.

Latimer Publications

Latimer Studies

LATIMER BRIEFINGS

Latimer Publications

LB06	Passion for the Gospel: Hugh Latimer (1485–1555) Then and Now. A commemorative lecture to mark the 450th anniversary of his martyrdom in Oxford	A. McGrath
LB07	Truth and Unity in Christian Fellowship	Michael Nazir-Ali
LB08	Unworthy Ministers: Donatism and Discipline Today	Mark Burkill
LB09	Witnessing to Western Muslims: A Worldview Approach to Sharing Faith	Richard Shumack
LB10	Scarf or Stole at Ordination? A Plea for the Evangelical Conscience	Andrew Atherstone
LB11	How to Write a Theology Essay	Michael P. Jensen
LB12	Preaching: A Guidebook for Beginners	Allan Chapple

Latimer Books

GGC	God, Gays and the Church: Human Sexuality and Experience in Christian Thinking	eds. Lisa Nolland, Chris Sugden, Sarah Finch
WTL	The Way, the Truth and the Life: Theological Resources for a Pilgrimage to a Global Anglican Future	eds. Vinay Samuel, Chris Sugden, Sarah Finch
AEID	Anglican Evangelical Identity – Yesterday and Today	J.I.Packer, N.T.Wright
IB	The Anglican Evangelical Doctrine of Infant Baptism	John Stott, Alec Motyer
BF	Being Faithful: The Shape of Historic Anglicanism Today	Theological Resource Group of GAFCON
TPG	The True Profession of the Gospel: Augustus Toplady and Reclaiming our Reformed Foundations	Lee Gatiss
SG	Shadow Gospel: Rowan Williams and the Anglican Communion Crisis	Charles Raven
TTB	Translating the Bible: From Willliam Tyndale to King James	Gerald Bray
PWS	Pilgrims, Warriors, and Servants: Puritan Wisdom for Today's Church	ed. Lee Gatiss
PPA	Preachers, Pastors, and Ambassadors: Puritan Wisdom for Today's Church	ed. Lee Gatiss
CWP	The Church, Women Bishops and Provision: The Integrity of Orthodox Objections to the Proposed Legislation Allowing Women Bishops	

Anglican Foundations Series

FWC	The Faith We Confess: An Exposition of the 39 Articles	Gerald Bray
AF02	The 'Very Pure Word of God': The Book of Common Prayer as a Model of Biblical Liturgy	Peter Adam
AF03	Dearly Beloved: Building God's People Through Morning and Evening Prayer	Mark Burkill
AF04	Day by Day: The Rhythm of the Bible in the Book of Common Prayer	Benjamin Sargent

Printed in Australia
AUOW01n0304260318
296032AU00002B/2

9 781906 327149